Fascination Concrete

Chris van Uffelen

Fascination Concrete

BRAUN

by Chris van Uffelen

Fascination Concrete

The fascination of concrete above all lies in its versatility: it is processed viscously, solid afterwards; it can span large distances, take on all conceivable shapes on site, cast or sprayed, but can also be placed as prefabricated bricks or elements; it changes its appearance with the aggregates, both in terms of fineness and color and in terms of feel; it can be highly compacted, relatively light, water-resistant or even translucent: concrete works in every case. Following the opus caementitium in the ancient Roman Empire, buildings were erected throughout the history of architecture by composite materials with additives that stuck between the outer shells – even if it was only clay and straw in historical half-timbered construction. Numerous ruins of medieval churches show that between brick shells only coarse stone, sometimes even scree and mortar was used, and even in Walter Gropius' famous Bauhaus building in Dessau (1926) is a lot material in the walls that one would not expect to find behind the perfect surface of a supposed concrete building.

The real history of modern concrete begins – after numerous experiments in the 19th century – with Auguste Perret's unpreserved dealer's garage in the Rue Ponthieu in Paris (1906/07), where concrete played a decisive role in the structure and appearance. Although various types of concrete had already been used in construction before, they were usually used somewhat bashfully as technically superior. For example in bridge construction or behind a facing of other materials concrete was kind of engineering requirement. With the Perret's garage and the buildings he subsequently designed, the French architect developed an aesthetic of concrete that Max Berg used to create an enormous vaulting at the Jahrhunderthalle in Wrocław (1913). Rudolf Steiner added the aspect of the modelled mass at the second Goetheanum in Dornach (1923). This aspect then played a rather subordinate role in classical modernism, for example in Expressionism, which already picked out the surfaces, while most leading architects, like those of Bauhaus and de Stijl, were enthusiastic about the possibility of working with thin orthogonal and linear forms.

After the Second World War their aesthetics remained dominant, but exposed concrete played an increasingly important role. Formwork holes, as an aesthetic grid, and the different tactile experience of different concrete surfaces became design elements. Only in Brutalism the mass and the large, deliberately shown aggregate did return. Exposed aggregate concrete showed the natural pebble and even in rough boarding, nature left its imprint in architecture. This was abandoned for cost reasons when individual formwork became too expensive, but now it is extremely popular again. A modern successor to this

Carel Visser: Salami, 1966. Exposed aggregate of the concrete sculpture in front of the university aula of the TU Delft.

are matrices, which, inserted into the formwork, leave behind extremely complex and very individual patterns. The character of such imprlnts is strongly dependent on the type of concrete used and – as this book shows – the whole range from fine to coarse is used for different tactile experiences.

Air inclusions are also part of the living surfaces. The expressionistic picking of the cast concrete surface, which brings the usually thicker and therefore enclosed aggregates to light, is also found again today. The same applies to the coloring of concrete, which not only looks nicer than a paint coat covering the material, but is also scratch-resistant.

Contemporary building uses both the thin and the voluminous character that the material can take on. The fact that both characters can be developed in both orthogonal and sculptural structures is also clearly visible in the examples of this volume. But besides these stylistic aspects, translucent concrete, 3D-printed concrete and knitcrete are also found as quite new material variants. This shows that the development of the material is far from exhausted.

by Oppenheim Architecture

The Ayla Clubhouse

The Ayla Golf Academy & Clubhouse takes inspiration from the natural dunes and mountains of the surrounding desert as well as the architectural heritage of the ancient Bedouin, who live in tents that are perfectly adapted to the harsh conditions of the desert. The distinct architectural form establishes a unique connection with nature by capturing the elemental, vibrant essence of the on the one hand hostile but on the other hand beautiful desert landscape. A massive concrete shell drapes over the program areas, enveloping the interior and exterior walls of each volume.

Location: Ayla Oasis, Aqaba, Jordan
Architect: Oppenheim Architecture
Year of Completion: 2018
Type of Concrete: shotcrete

East elevation

West elevation

Ground floor plan

View from southeast

Two "comfort stations" are hosting cafes and restrooms for the golfers

View from west

Screen detail

Interior view

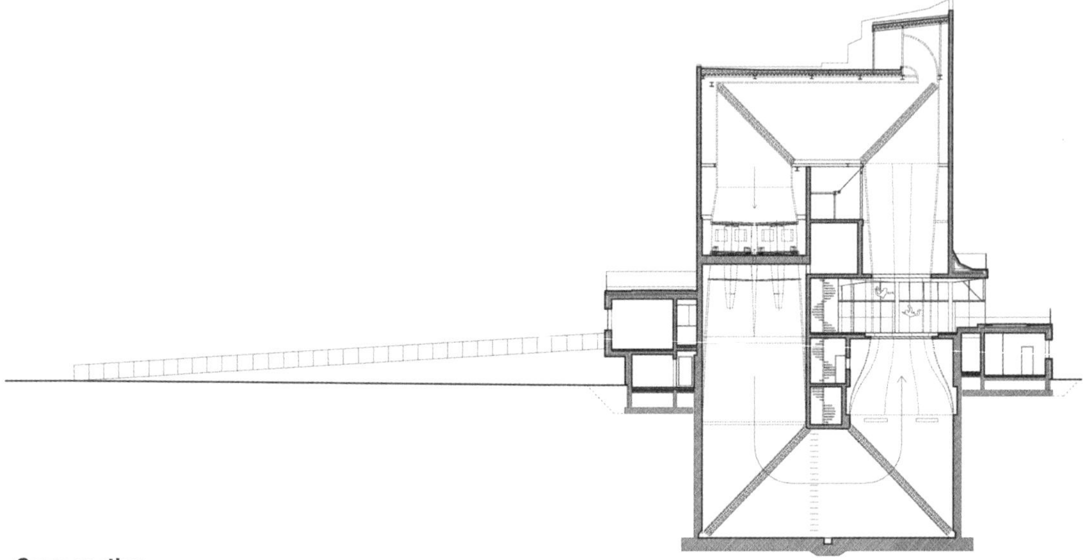

Cross section

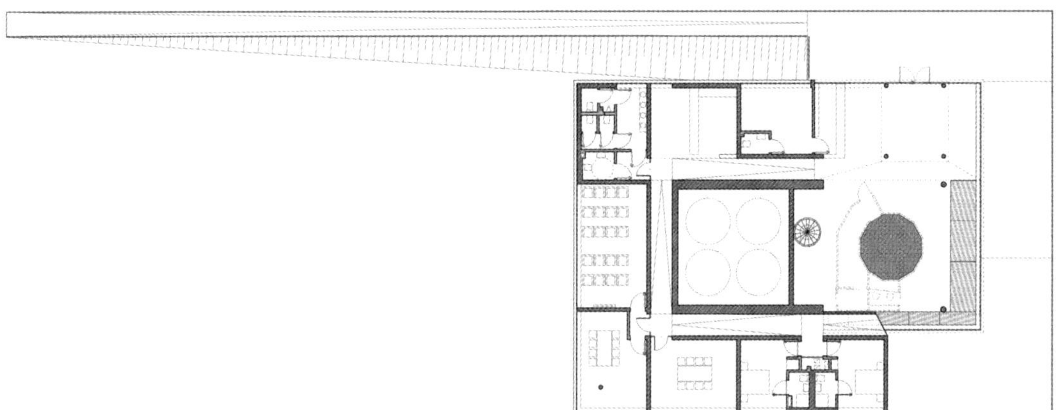

First floor plan

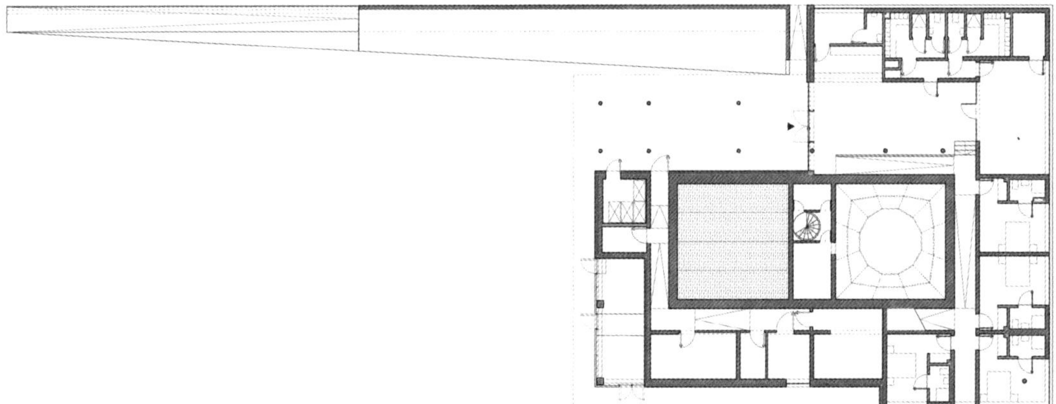

Ground floor plan

by Biuro Projektów Lewicki Łatak

Flyspot Warsaw

The wind tunnel building consists of an internal volume having the shape of a cylindrical tube, formed by a square. The tube contains the core technology of the vertical wind tunnel. Around the tube, there are different, spirally arranged spaces including: the reception, office and hotel rooms, conference facilities, bathrooms, changing rooms. All these spaces are connected through the entrance hall using the inclined corridor, which ascends gradually leading to the flying hall. This is where the key feature of the building is located, the glass cylinder, which forms part of the cubature. Inside the cylinder, powerful units generate wind moving upwards to 300 kilometers per hour, lifting visitors up to more than a dozen meters. Indoor skydiving and the associations with floating kites were the key inspiration in designing the external form of the building.

Location: Mory, Poland
Architect: Biuro Projektów Lewicki Łatak
Year of Completion: 2014
Type of Concrete: in-situ concrete

West façade detail

East façade detail

View from north

West façade detail with landscape

View from east

View from north by night

East façade detail

by Alexander Brenner Architekten

Brenner Research House PR39

The house as a building block of the city should be a sign of durability and solidity. Through the coarse pointing of the concrete skin it looks like a rock and at the same time it gets a high degree of fineness and precision through the stonemasonry-like scratching of the edges and parapets. All materials used on and in the house are characterized by their natural, untreated and unsealed surfaces. Concrete, wood, steel, lime plaster and other natural materials create an authentic feeling of space. The prominent location of the house allows a beautiful view on the city of Stuttgart.

Location: Stuttgart, Germany
Architect: Alexander Brenner Architekten
Year of Completion: 2019
Type of Concrete: exposed concrete

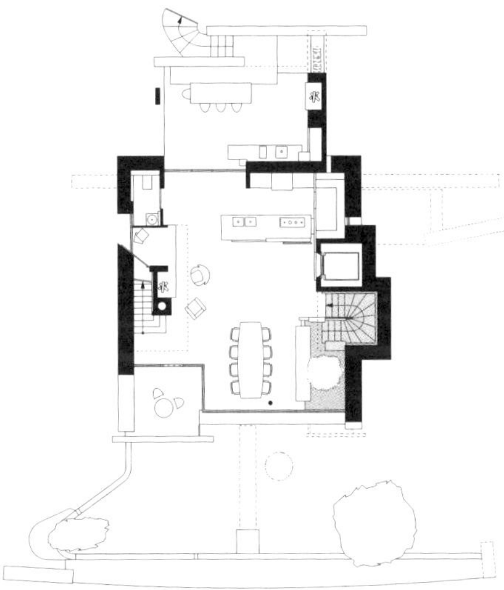

Fourth floor plan

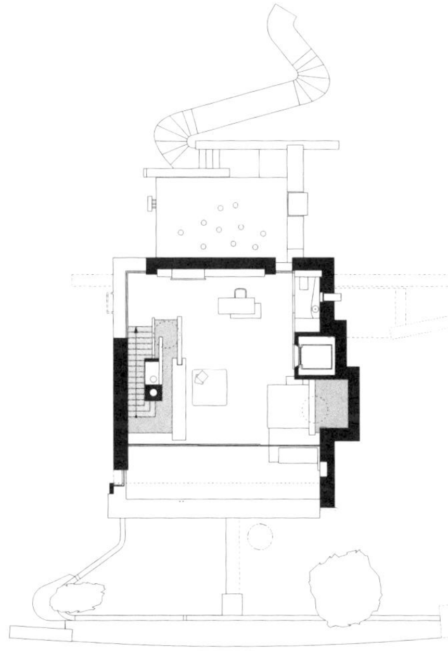

Fifth floor plan

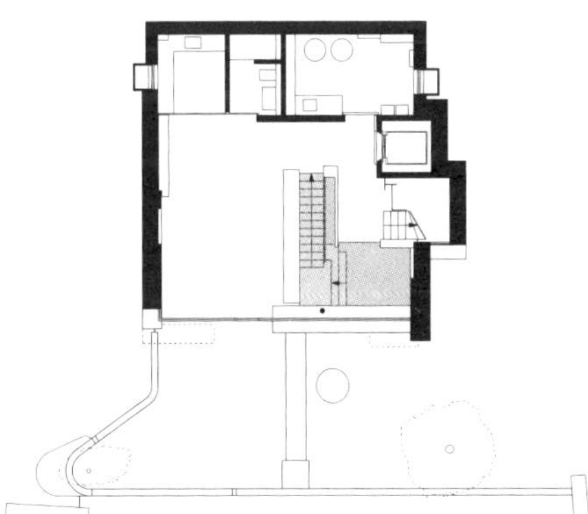

First floor plan

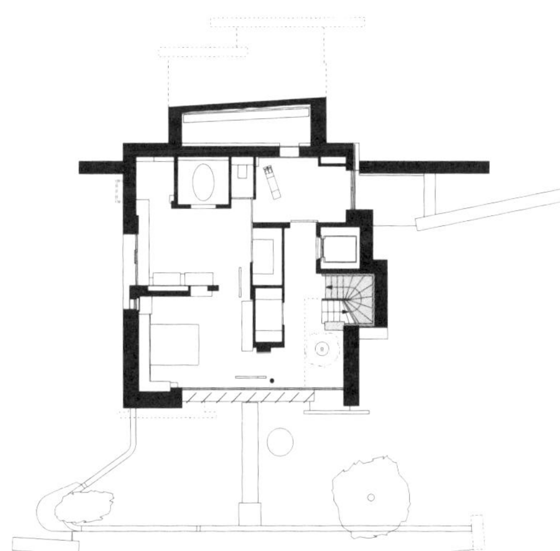

Second floor plan

Street view from southeast

Kitchen terrace

Kitchen counter with a base made of concrete

Entrance hall

Concrete couch and terrace with pergola

View from northwest

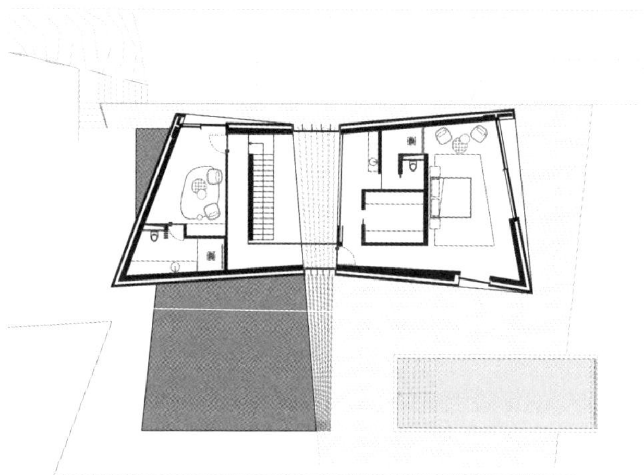

First floor plan

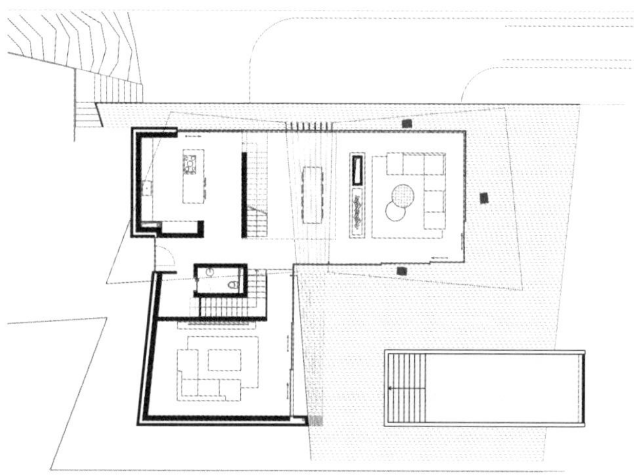

Ground floor plan

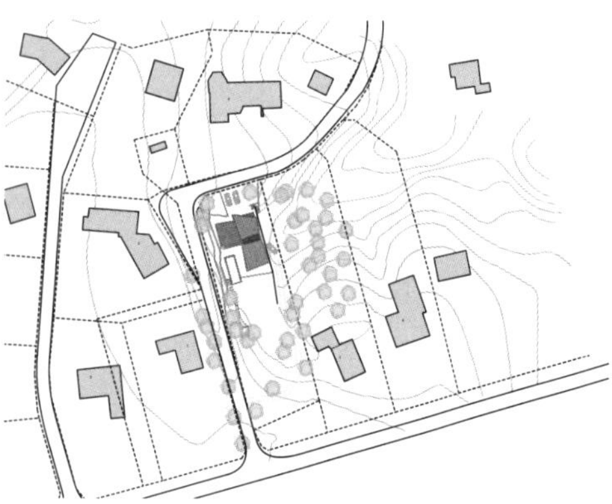

Site plan

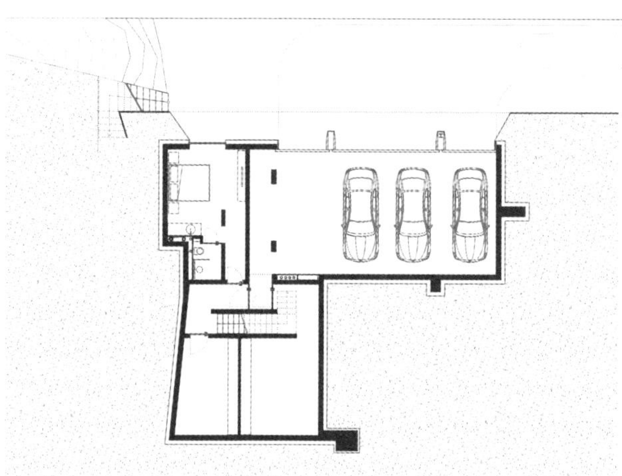

Basement floor plan

by Querkopf Architekten

Villa NEO

Villa NEO presents itself minimalistic but at the same time full of distinctive trademarks. The building made out of exposed concrete stands on a natural stone basement. Closed concrete walls surrounding the entrance create a comfortable, protected feeling and lead to the southern side. Large windows on that side of the house offer exceptional views of the surrounding woods. The central living space connects all rooms located on the ground floor to a broad, open area. Meanwhile the upper floor focuses on privacy. With its imposing, twisted volume this area creates a bright space with a very characteristic look.

Location: Rosengarten, Germany
Architect: Querkopf Architekten
Year of Completion: 2019
Type of Concrete: in-situ concrete

View from north

Living room

Garden view

Bedroom

by Touch Architect

Option Coffee Bar

The Option Coffee Bar consists of the main areas cafe, restaurant and bar. These can be extended or supplemented on a part-time basis with the following secondary functions: cafe, bakery and healthy food restaurant in the morning or craft beer bar in the evening. There are two floors fitted in a rectangular, functional box: the first floor with cafe and counter bar, and the mezzanine floor for customers' seats only. The simple white box was created to contrast the surroundings, together with focusing on art elements inside. The white box comes together with two types of voids, which are either transparent or translucent. The translucent element is the central element of the front façade and is made of double-layer clear-color polycarbonate which creates variation of light.

Location: Mueang, Udon Thani, Thailand
Architect: Touch Architect
Year of Completion: 2019
Type of Concrete: lightweight concrete

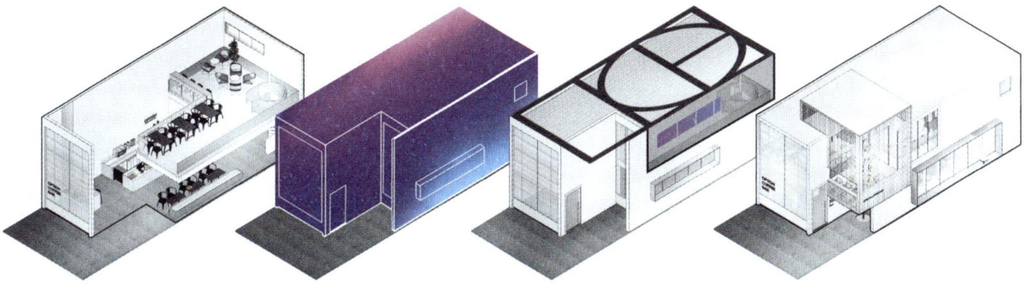

Different forms of usage

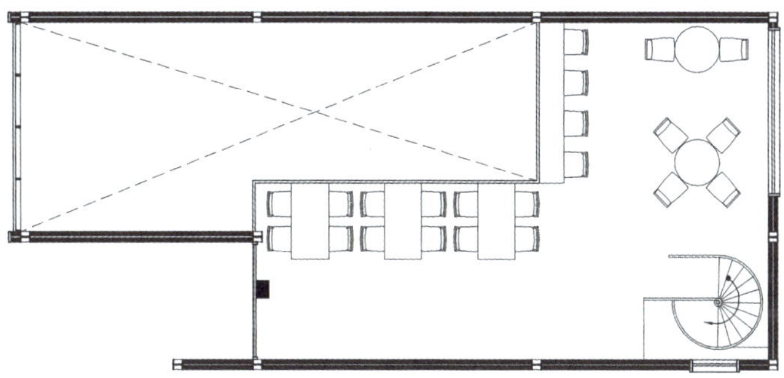

First floor plan

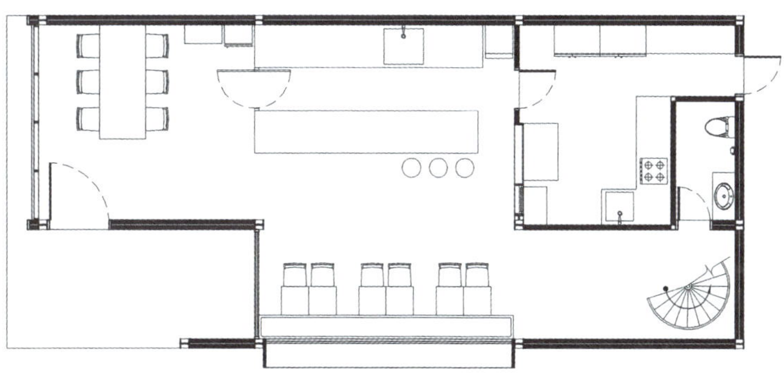

Ground floor plan

Longitudinal section

First floor exhibition space

Coffee bar

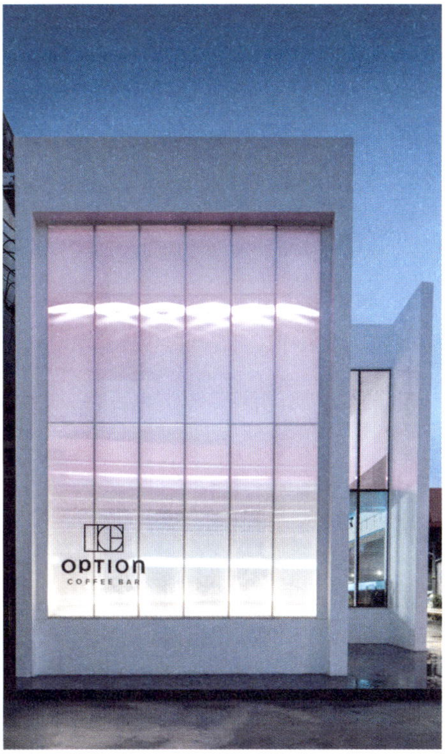

Frontal view

Longitudinal view

Transformation from cafe to bar

Top floor plan

Third floor plan

Second floor plan

First floor plan

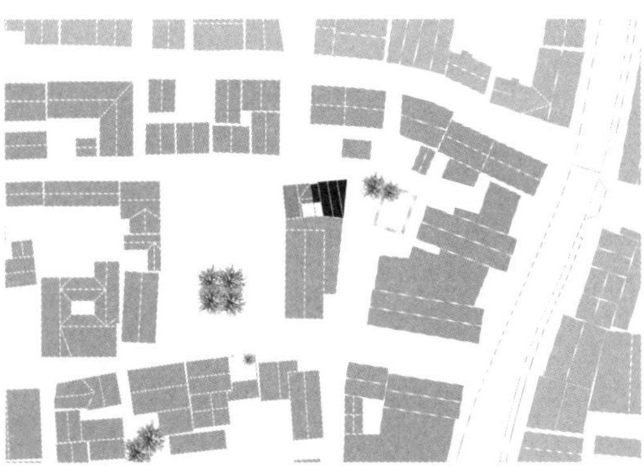

Site plan

Ground floor plan

by hochstrasser.architekten

K5

The cubature of the building, as well as the orientation of the roof are inspired by the surrounding gabled houses. Another lead to the regional, historical architecture are the materials used during the building process, for example the wooden window frames or the exposed concrete as a hint at the traditional usage of stone and wood. Because of the small property as well as the difficult thermal insulation value regulations the architects had to be flexible, these circumstances lead to the decision for light concrete and foam glass ballast as the main building materials. Due to static reasons the ground floor was build monolithically, while the upper floors were poured in one piece. With its fascinating architecture and the different functions of the k5, it's a likely used place to meet friends, relax or work.

Location: Ulm, Germany
Architect: hochstrasser.architekten
Year of Completion: 2016
Type of Concrete: insulating concrete

Window detail

Staircase detail

Exposed concrete detail

Street view

Main office room

Façade detail

Office room

by Architect-K

Songdo House

The curvy shape of the Songdo House was inspired by the Busan city alleys, perfectly adapting to the irregular architectural style typical for the city. Each floor offers individual spaces and programs, flowing with the special shape of the house. Eight stairs lead to various connections between the different floor levels and an additional tube bridge gains comfort and the possibility to create new routes through the building. The materials used, exposed concrete with bamboo or pine formwork, wood and basalt bricks and metal panels, provide the circulation flow in the building and highlight the different alleys in the spaces. The rooms in Songdo House are named Dependent-Independent Spaces because they are not traditional, but defined by other elements.

Location: Busan, Republic of Korea
Architect: Architect-K
Year of Completion: 2014
Type of Concrete: exposed concrete

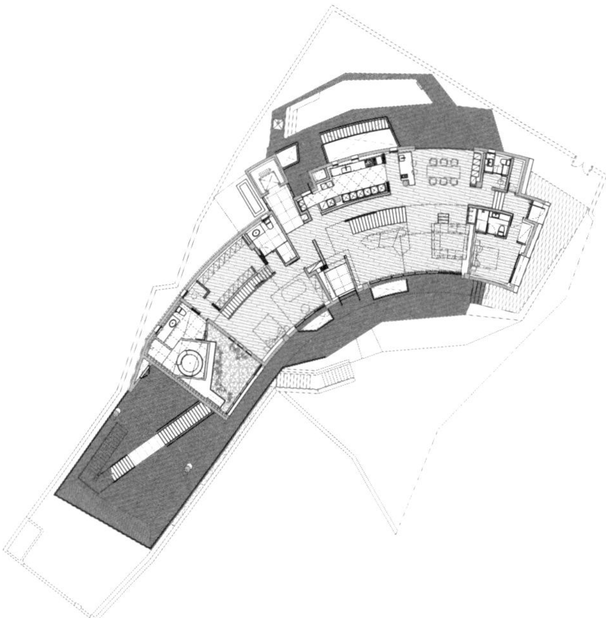

First floor plan

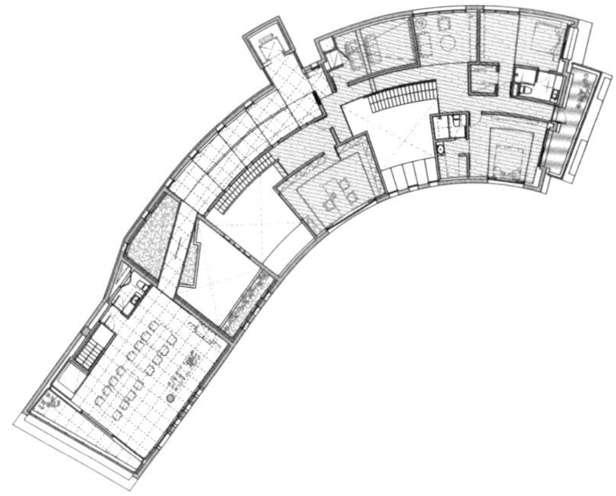

Second floor plan

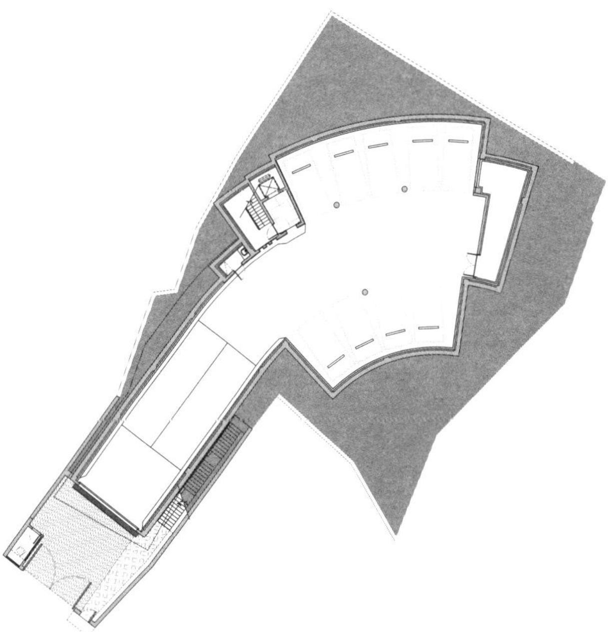

Basement floor plan

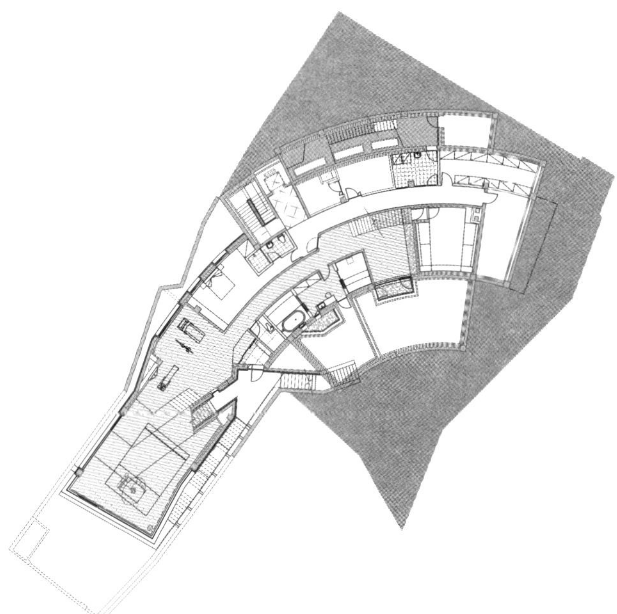

Ground floor plan

Bird's-eye view

Internal garden

Cantilevering stairs

Living room

Bathroom with internal garden

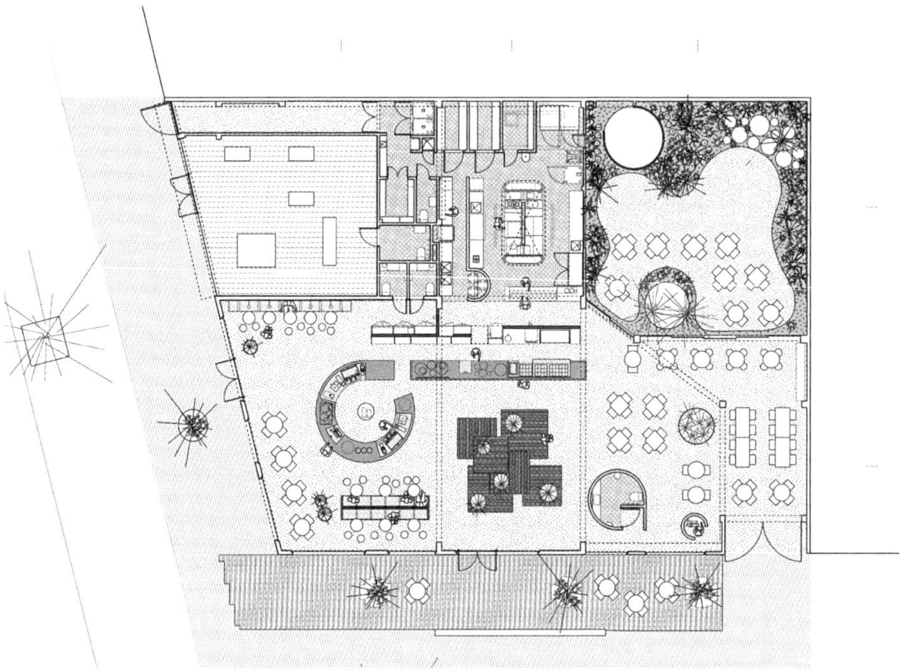

Ground floor plan

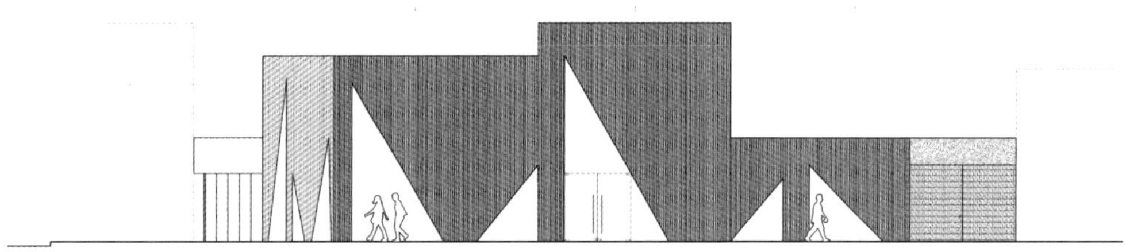

Longitudinal view

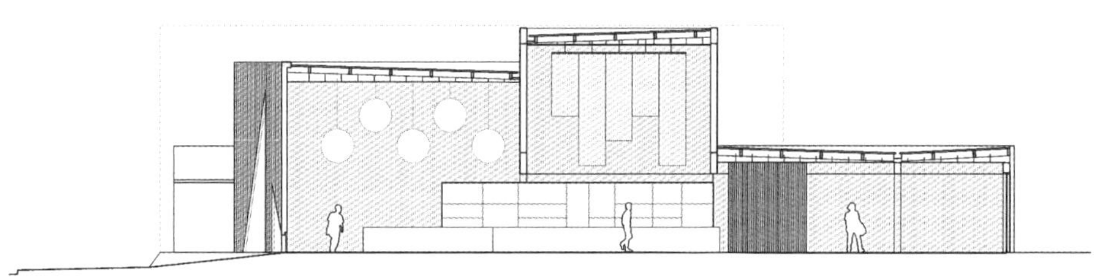

Cross section

by Studio Cadena

Masa Cafe & Bakery

Organized as a grouping of distinct but interconnected volumes, this building houses a cafe, a bakery, and a retail space on a corner lot in a residential neighborhood of Bogota. Using simple forms and materials to maximize the effect of the building, it articulates spaces, textures, and light to deliver multiple environments with unique character. Large triangular windows, cut into the building's textured concrete walls, open the façade to the street while revealing the life within. The design shapes a new place in the city with a unique character that is memorable at the urban scale yet remains rooted to its surrounding context, not by how it looks, but rather, how it works inside and out.

Location: Bogota, Colombia
Architect: Studio Cadena
Year of Completion: 2018
Type of Concrete: in-situ concrete

Street view

Window detail

Seating options

Patio with seating option

Checkout area

by Atelier Stéphane Fernandez

Center for Oceanological Research

A rectangular monolith faced entirely in a coral-pink cladding, the project overlooks the marina and is a landmark of the town's waterfront. Behind this undulating wrapping we find the minimalist form of the main body of residential rooms, defined by a peripheral layout: walkways that are both balconies and access to the accommodation. On the first floor, the restaurant is located and its presence is indicated with a large gash in the coral wrapping, allowing a great view at the sea. This regular volume is set on a massive plinth eroded in an unusual way by concrete caves, in the middle of which the main entrance is cut. Hosting a residence with 75 apartments for short-term stays for students and researchers, the building complex also includes a catering space for all users of the observatory.

Location: Banyuls-sur-Mer, France
Architect: Atelier Stéphane Fernandez
Year of Completion: 2015
Type of Concrete: red reinforced concrete

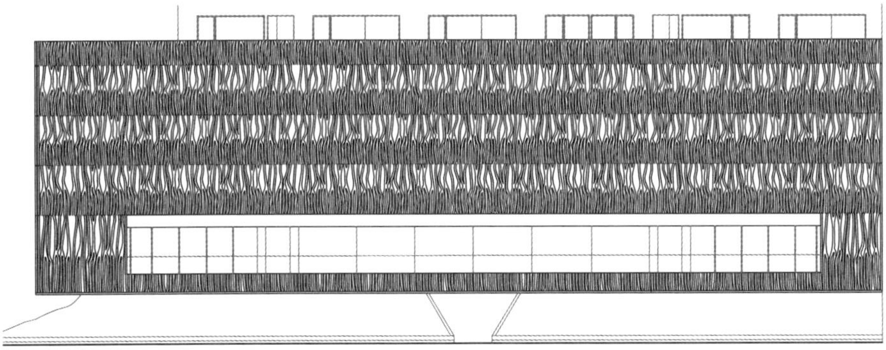

Elevation

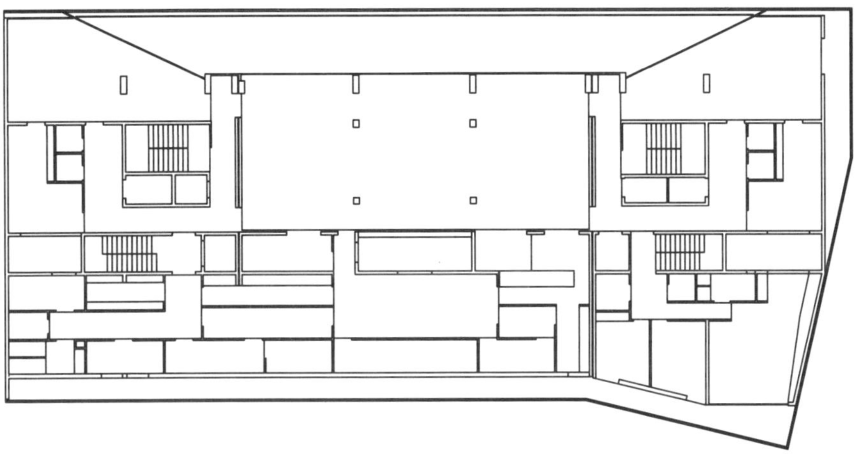

Ground floor plan

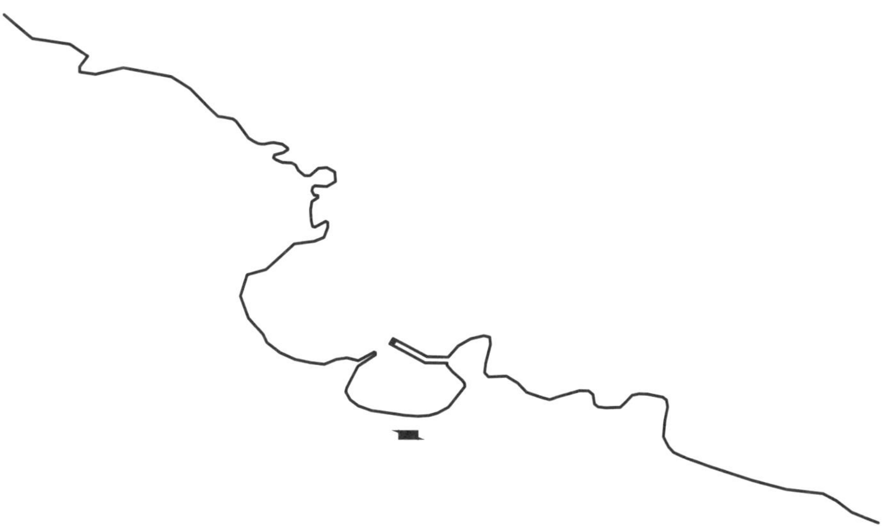

Situation

Parking area view

Street view

Façade detail

Street view from the side

Inside the corridor

Port view

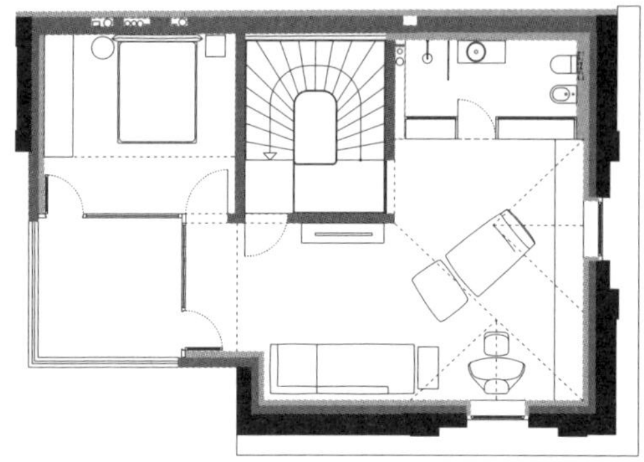

Second floor plan

Cross section

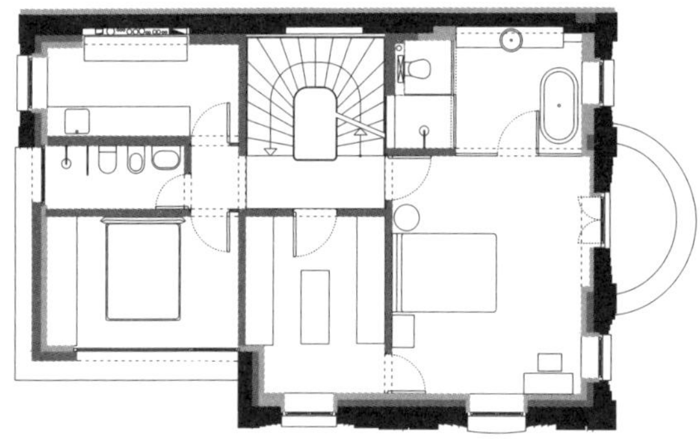

First floor plan

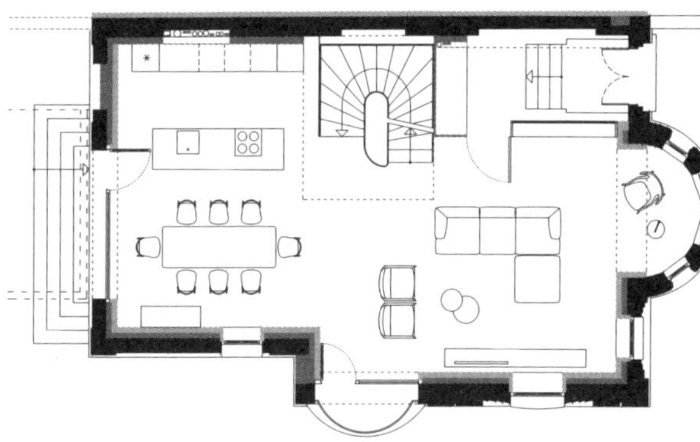

Ground floor plan

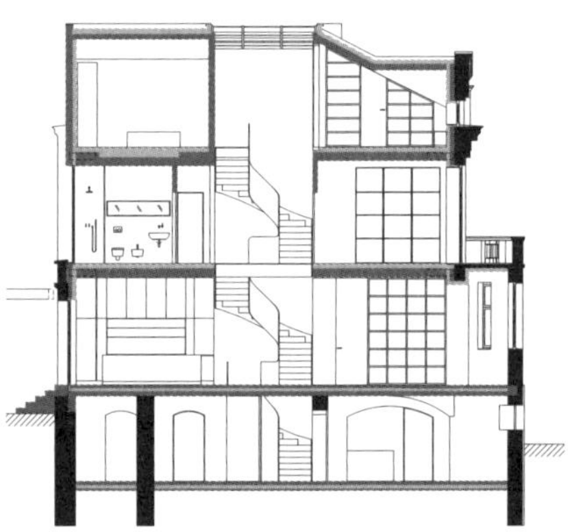

Longitudinal section

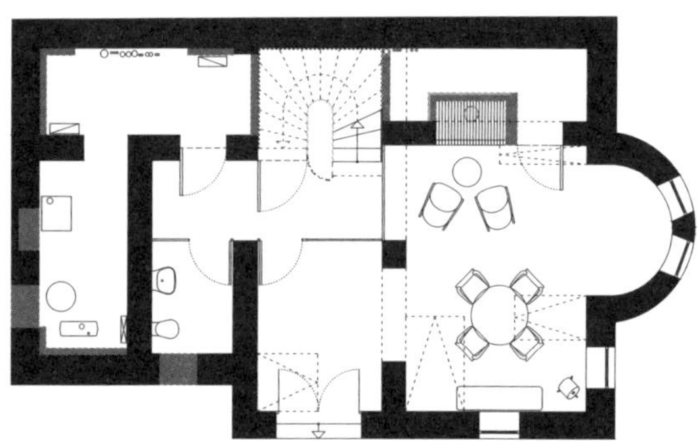

Basement floor plan

by I/O architects

White Concrete Old House

This house from the 1920s was a romantic ruin surrounded by authentic and new-built fragments of ancient Augusta Traiana and rather isolated from the contemporary city, yet in its very center. The idea behind the whole reconstruction process, was to design a contemporary interpretation of the avant-garde architecture. A new volume of white concrete complements the structure and the program of the old house.

Location: Stara Zagora, Bulgaria
Architect: I/O architects
Year of Completion: 2017
Type of Concrete: white in-situ concrete

The composition of the openings, the ambiguous elements of the addition and used materials lead to the two distinctive identities of the building. Through the bright and open design of the new stairs, the whole house develops a comfortable and warm atmosphere. The new glossy white concrete slabs integrate and conceal all the contemporary technology of the house.

Garden view

Outdoor kitchen and patio

Garden view at dusk

Master bedroom

Living area

Entrance

Surrounding city

by hehnpohl architektur

House at the Buddenturm

Similar to the "City at the Edge of the World" by Lyonel Feininger, the building, located in the historic city of Münster, shows a collective typology with the houses surrounding it. Three openings mark the façade facing the street, the copper façade at the ground floor and the two upper floors with glazed incisions, which allow a far view down the street to the Buddenturm. The staggered façade also creates the diversified staircase in the interior, which widens each floor to absorb as much daylight from the roof glazing as possible. Organized by four floors, the first level contains kitchen, terrace, living and dining room and is the main lounge. Garage and entree are located on the ground floor while bathrooms and bedrooms spread over the remaining two floors.

Location: Münster, Germany
Architect: hehnpohl architektur
Year of Completion: 2018
Type of Concrete: in-situ concrete

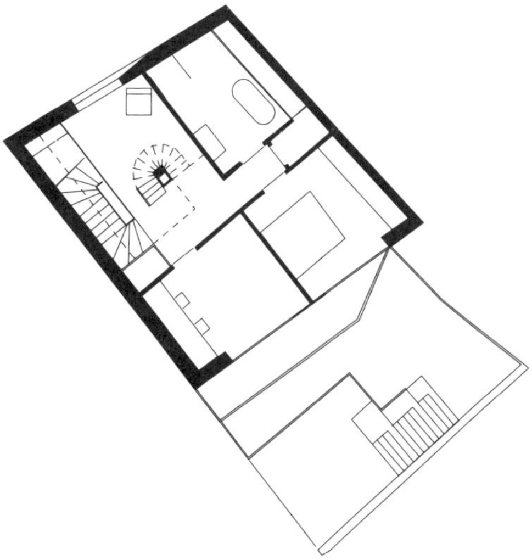

Second floor plan

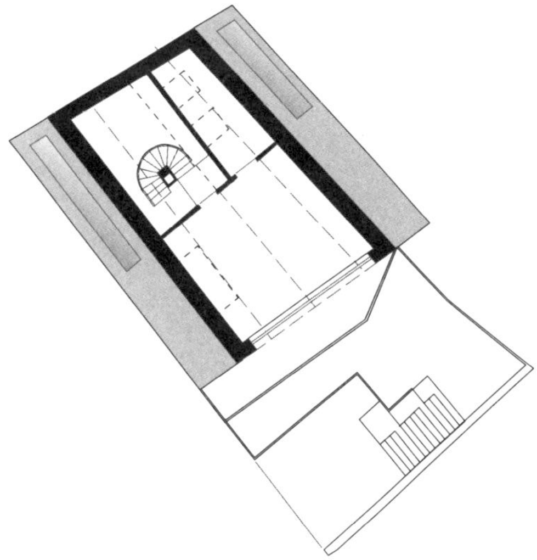

Top floor plan

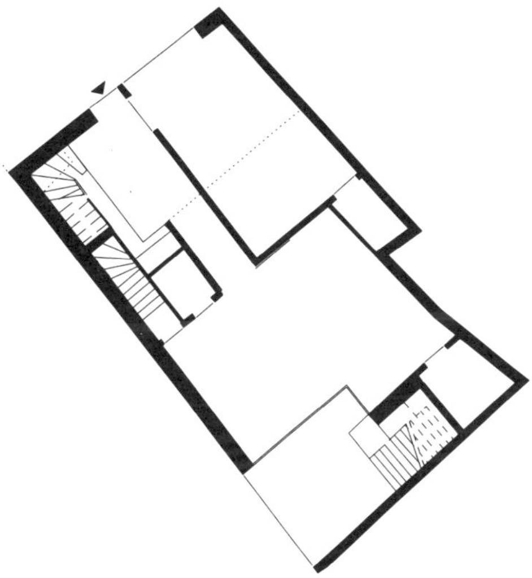

Ground floor plan

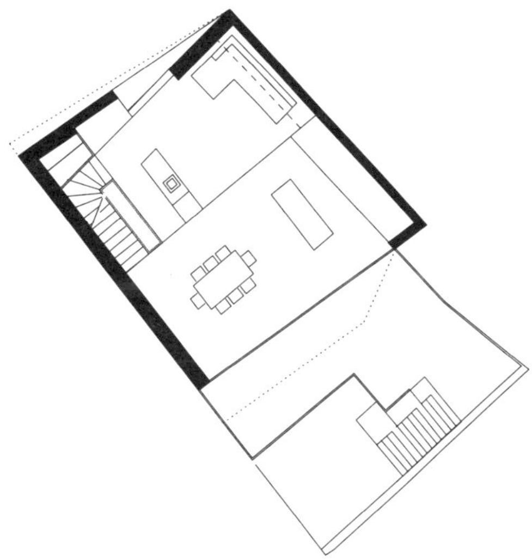

First floor plan

Sketch façade

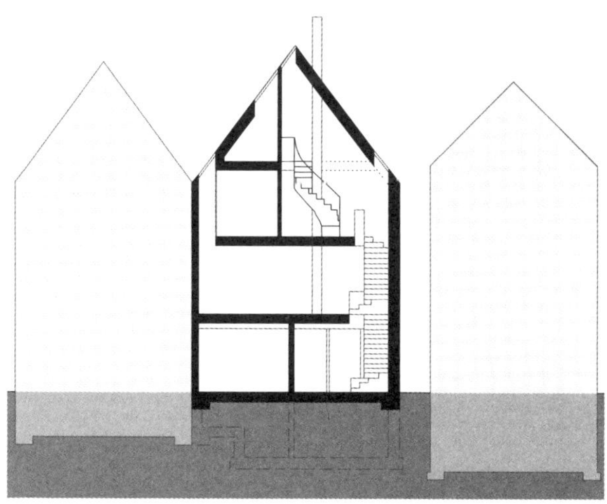

Cross section

Kitchen

Roof ridge and eave

Staircase

Spiral staircase

Seating position second floor

Patio

Tamped black concrete at the wall

View by night

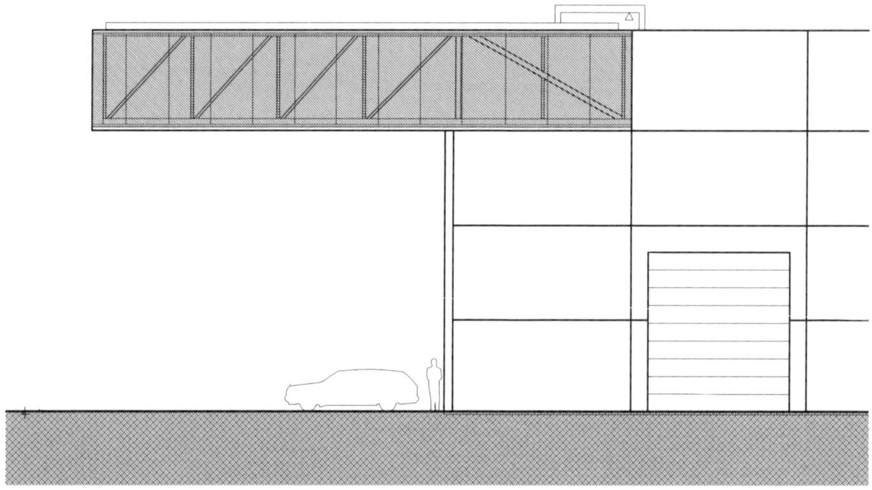

Elevation

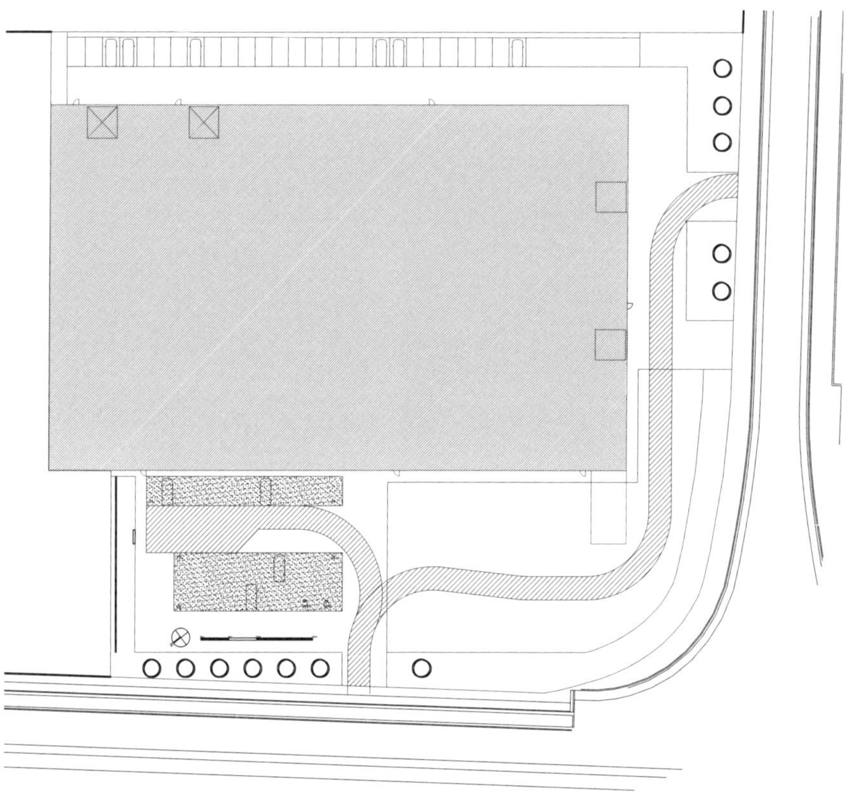

Ground floor plan

by Govaert & Vanhoutte Architects

Enjoy Concrete

The building mainly consists of a hall for production and storage. The office spaces are in front of the building, spread over four levels, allowing light and visibility onto the main road. A cantilevered volume containing the boardroom is located at the top corner of the building. The long volume was made out of a lighter steel structure, allowing large windows on the southwest façade. The steel structure is internally anchored into the concrete staircase, creating a counterweight for the long cantilever. Inside the boardroom a solid steel table stands only on two legs. The façade is further characterized by a pattern image of the beautiful treeline along the canal Damse Vaart on the prefabricated slabs through the application of the "graphic concrete" procedure. The digital image was broken down into big dots, making the total picture become clear only from a distance.

Location: Veurne, Belgium
Architect: Govaert & Vanhoutte Architects
Year of Completion: 2010
Type of Concrete: "graphic concrete"

Façade with windows

Façade detail

Entrance area

Office space

The façade creates an interesting interaction between the building and its surroundings

View at night

by Schulz und Schulz

Building N

The building N (Gebäude N) carefully replenishes the old campus structure from the sixties and seventies, putting the strict and orthogonal structure of the historic campus in a modern context. Inspired by the existing architecture the new building is wrapped in a ribbon window façade with curtained ready-mix concrete. The ribbon windows are clad with surface flush, vertical rotatable metal lamellae, which realize different changeable light and viewing situations. The interior is designed as an open areal, through a central communication space all four main floors of the building complex are connected and float into each other, creating an open room for discussions and scientific exchange.

Location: Karlsruhe, Germany
Architect: Schulz und Schulz
Year of Completion: 2017
Type of Concrete: ready-mix concrete

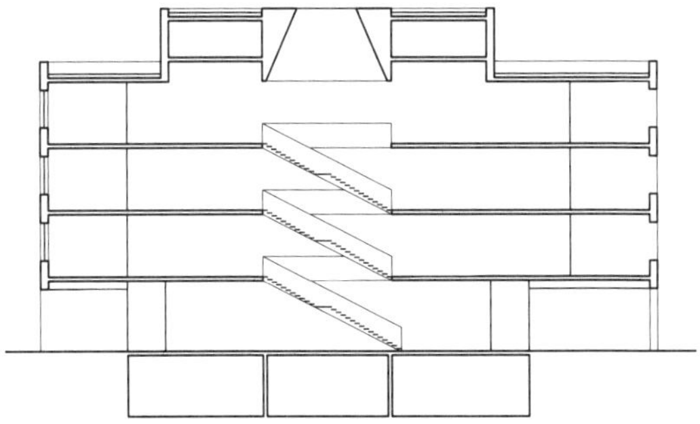

Cross section

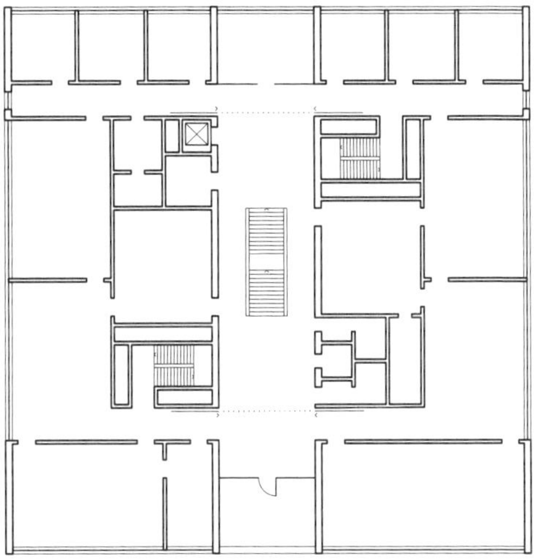

First floor plan

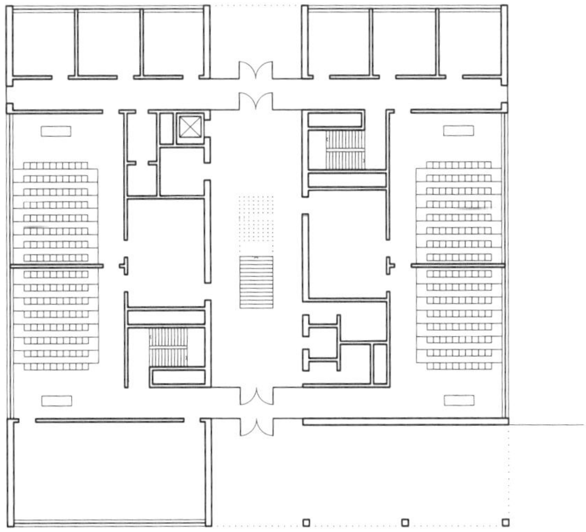

Ground floor plan

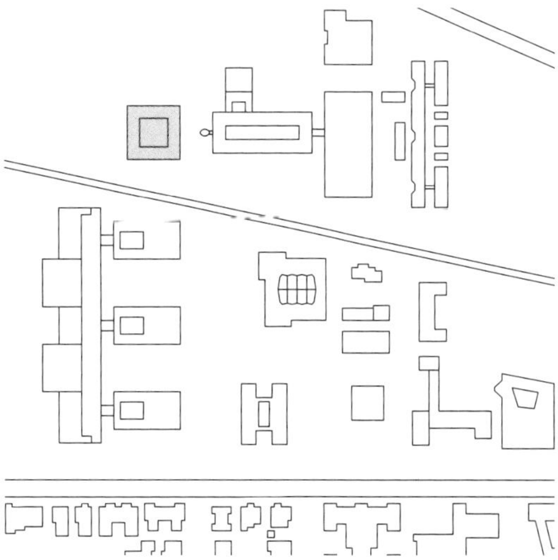

Site plan

Exterior view

Fingerprint on the façade

Stairs to the upper floors

Lecture hall

Laboratory

Façade detail

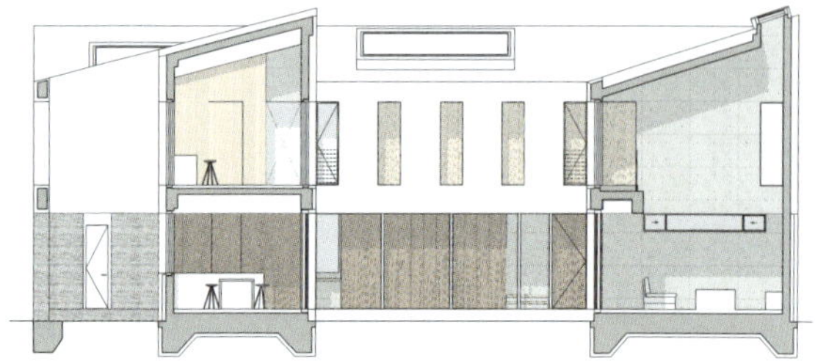

Cross section

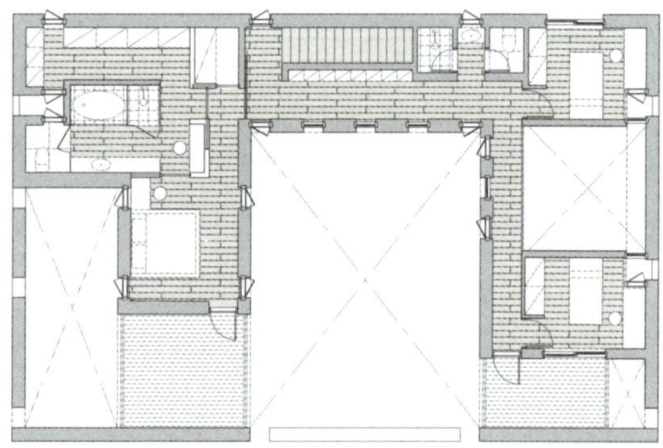

First floor plan

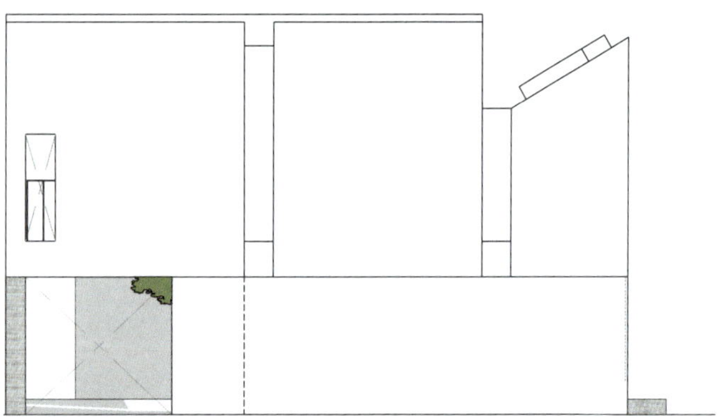

Elevation

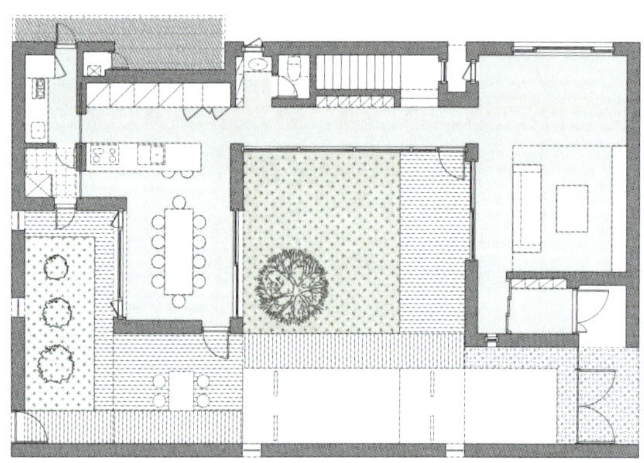

Ground floor plan

by Architect-K

Triangle Rectangle House

The intensity of modern city life leads to new architectural challenges, combining the social aspect of housing and the striving for a calm and relaxing environment. To create as much privacy as possible, the house was built around a spacious inner courtyard. Large open spaces and the connection between inside and outside, create a constant circulation within the building. Carefully manufactured apertures hem the façade, allowing views in the surrounding landscape but still maintain the privacy of the inhabitants. Due to the shape of the apertures, each hour of the day creates a different atmosphere, filling the space with different lighting situations. The numerous exposed concrete walls develop into plain canvases, newly painted each day by the sun rays.

Location: Yangsan-si, Republic of Korea
Architect: Architect-K
Year of Completion: 2019
Type of Concrete: exposed concrete

Living area with courtyard

Staircase

Living room

Bathroom by daylight

Stairs view with lighting

Street view

by Atelier Martel

Hôpital Suisse

For the restructuring and extension of the Hôpital Suisse the architects proposed a rational and functional project that reinforces the institution's image. The design for the extension follows the structural logic of the main building by simplifying its façade, thereby displaying the hierarchy between the two buildings with a degree of reverence that tones down the contrasts to highlight a spatial and historic continuity. Like the first building the structure of the extension is composed of a white exoskeleton. Contemporary preoccupations led the architects to reflect on working with the concrete mass, in a demonstration of the possibility to respect stringent thermal regulations without sacrificing quality of expression. A belvedere garden on the roof, which houses a restaurant, offers breathtaking views over Paris and the surrounding parks.

Location: Issy-les-Moulineaux, France
Architect: Atelier Martel
Year of Completion: 2016
Type of Concrete: precast concrete

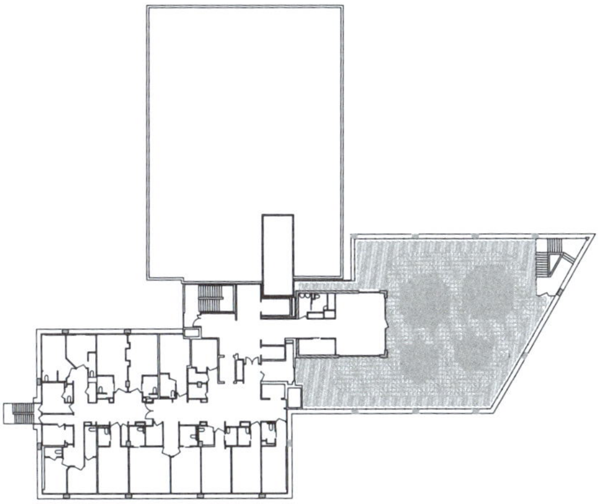

Second floor plan

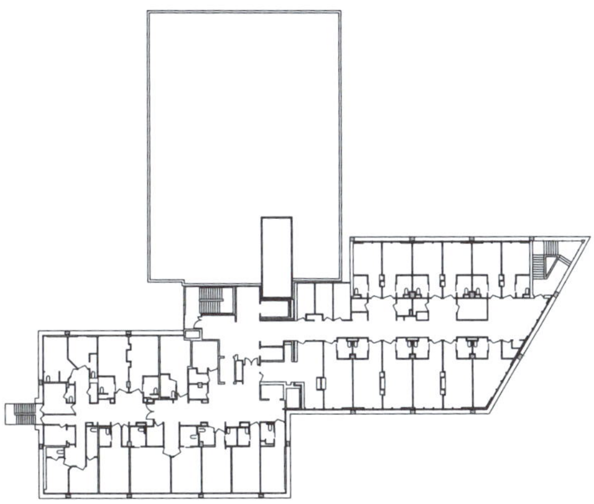

First floor plan

Site plan

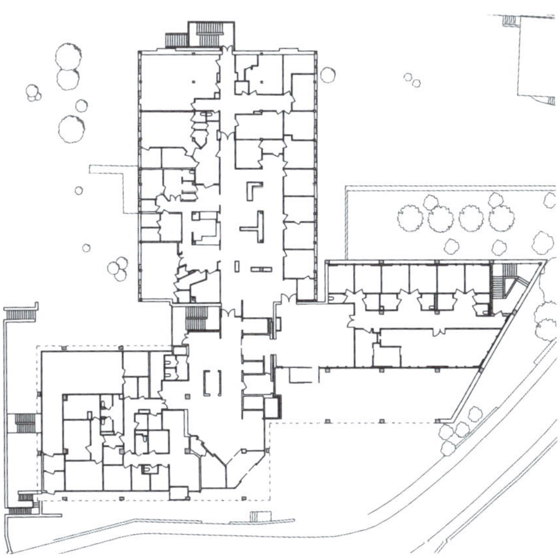

Ground floor plan

The new wing of the hospital and its connection with the original building

Façade detail

View from one of the rooms

View from the neighboring park

The belvedere garden with artistic intervention by Catherine Bolle

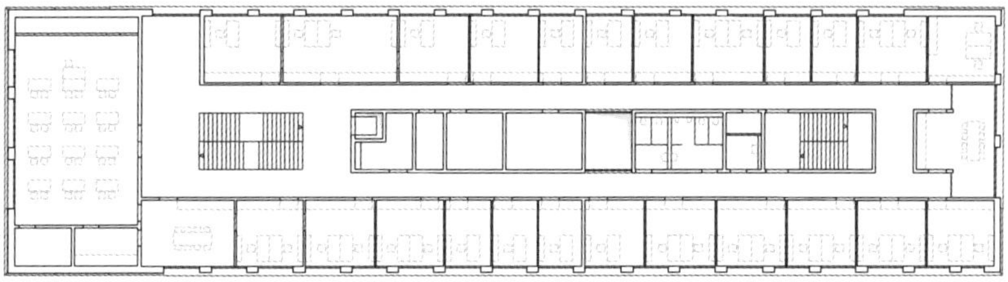

First floor plan

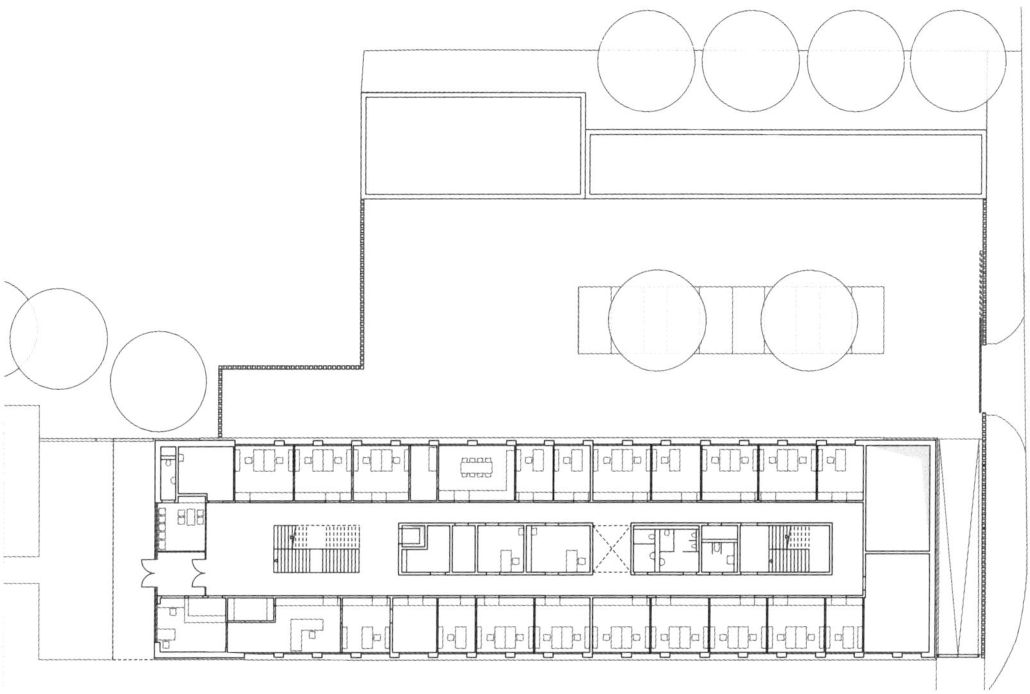

Ground floor plan

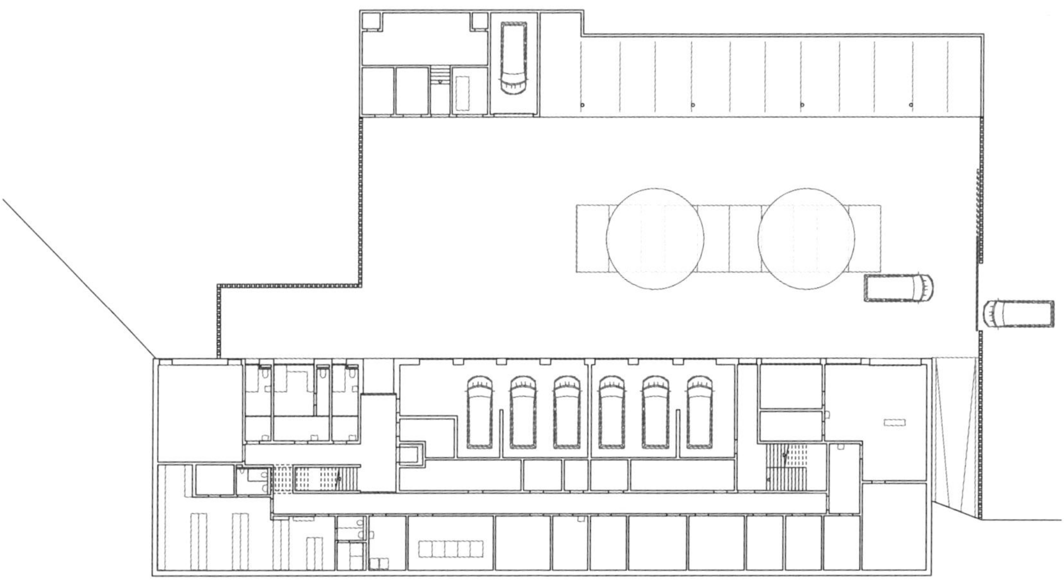

Basement floor plan

by Bez + Kock Architekten

Traffic Police Service Aschaffenburg

The Traffic Police Service Aschaffenburg is located on a plot of land that gently slopes downhill. Taking advantage of the topography, the offices are housed in a two-story block with ground level access. This is located on a dark plinth floor, which is only visible from the valley side and accommodates the adjoining rooms. The elongated structure has a façade of white through-dyed precast concrete elements. Its fine relief is emphasized by the slightly shiny surface of the acidified concrete. The compact, three-flush floor plan is enriched by rooflight situations.

Location: Aschaffenburg, Germany
Architect: Bez + Kock Architekten
Year of Completion: 2018
Type of Concrete: precast concrete

West façade with entrance

East façade

Detail north façade

Stairs near the main entrance

by Diego Guidotti Architetto

Residenza al Colle

The Residenza al Colle, a clear and compact volume, lies along Vacallo's main road in line with the existing facilities. The plinth building is a multi-family house, containing parking areas and different utility spaces. Three floors offer six different apartments that are supplemented through galleries, which enlarge the rear façade and connect the living space with the surrounding garden areal. Covered terraces act as common meeting places, used for garden parties and short chats. Terraces and garden are linked via an exterior bridge, allowing a smooth transition between the concrete architecture and nature. The two completely different façades reflect the environment Residenza al Colle is situated in, the façade facing the street is rather urban, dark and closed, whereas the opposing garden side opens itself with big windows and bright white color.

Location: Vacallo, Switzerland
Architect: Diego Guidotti Architetto
Year of Completion: 2017
Type of Concrete: in-situ concrete

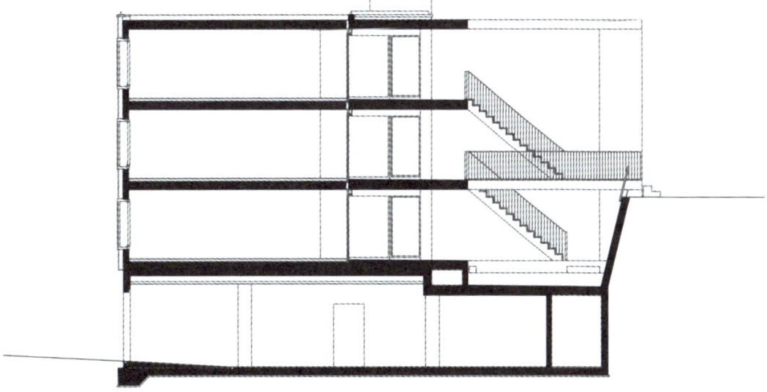

Cross section

First floor plan

Ground floor plan

Site plan

Garden view

Apartment door with adjoining gallery

Exterior area ground floor

Street view

Garden view

Garden path

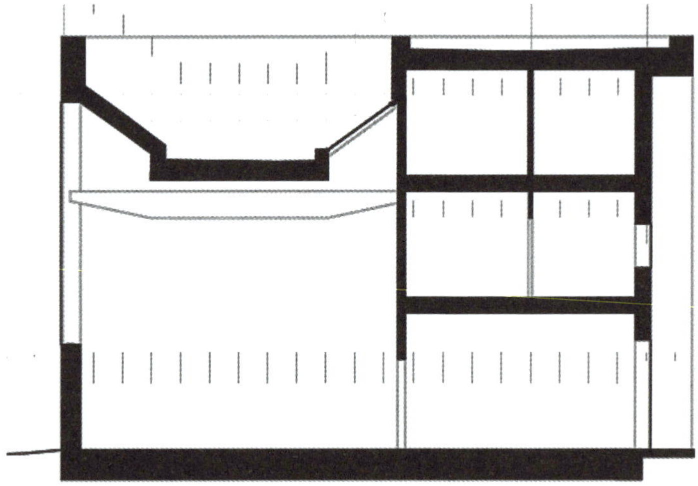

Cross section

Site plan

by kister scheithauer gross, Prof. Susanne Gross

Gerhard Pahl Center, TU Darmstadt

The Gerhard Pahl Center is more than a modular, flexible and clearly zoned hall of the Technical University (TU). The natural lighting via two light sources and the suspended ceiling beams create a play between structural mass, lightness and mobility in the large hall volume. The centrally located hall is conceived as a spatial body that continuously captures a maximum amount of daylight from two light sources. The massive concrete girders are tapered at the intersections with the outer wall by means of coving and do not rest on the wall but are connected to it in a suspended manner. The institute building blends in terms of content and form into the existing structure of the institute buildings. The teaching center was planned with a monolithic fair-faced precast concrete façade, in contrast, the office area was given a curtain-type, rear-ventilated metal façade.

Location: Darmstadt, Germany
Architect: kister scheithauer gross, Prof. Susanne Gross
Year of Completion: 2017
Type of Concrete: reinforced concrete

Façade detail

Interior of the hall

Weight-bearing construction with reinforced concrete

Entrance

by Inches Geleta

Palazzo Pioda

Boundary distances and building laws determine the volume of the building. Extending over six stories, the palazzo houses one apartment per floor and is a hybrid construction. On the one hand, it shows its dignity and urban integrity by turning the load-bearing structure outwards, thus determining the façade, while on the other hand, the prefabricated façade elements made of perforated sheet metal do not negate the semi-industrial and handcrafted character of the place. The architecture of the Palazzo Pioda responds to the dynamics of its setting by recalling the integrity of a modernist expression and thus creates a dialogue with the old Tendenza masters from the Ticino region.

Location: Locarno, Switzerland
Architect: Inches Geleta
Year of Completion: 2018
Type of Concrete: lightweight concrete

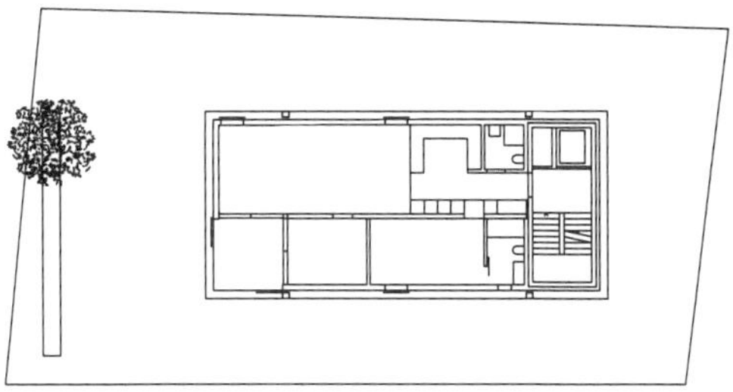

First floor plan

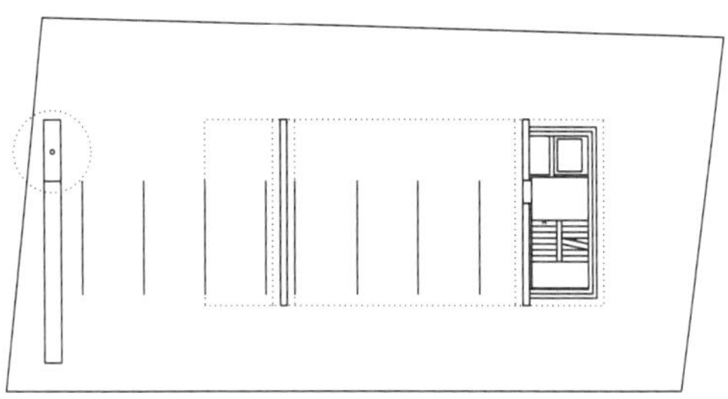

Ground floor plan

Site plan

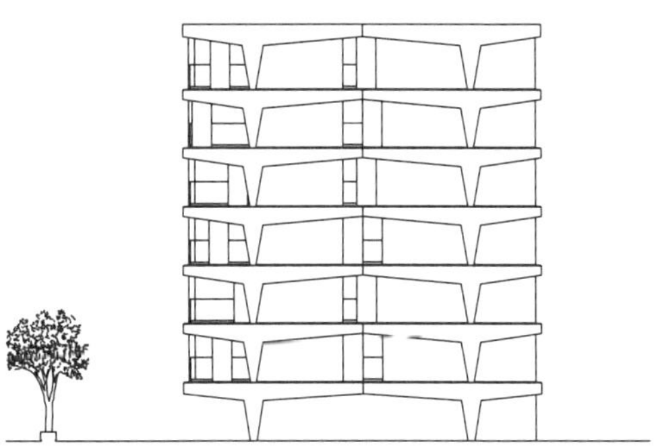

Longitudinal elevation

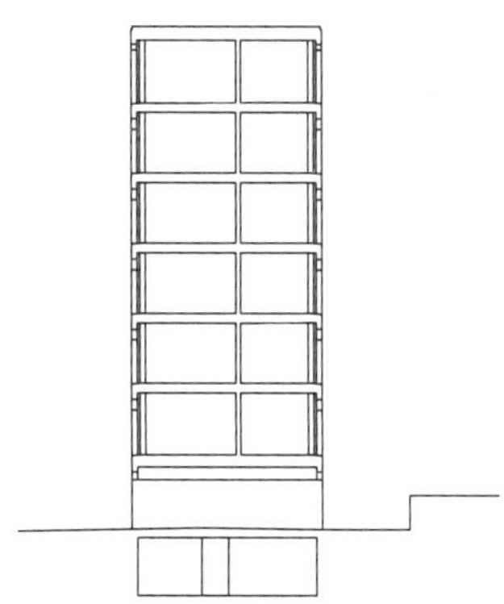

Cross section

New urban identity for a dense area

The building shows urban integrity by turning the load-bearing structure outwards

Exterior design

Interior view

Interior design

Interior view

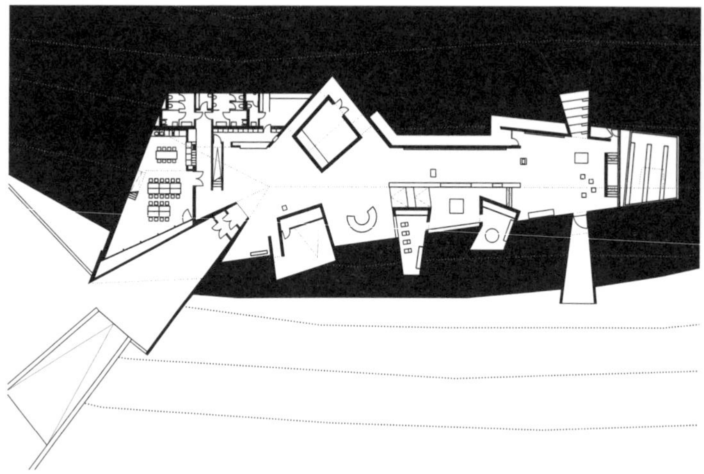

Ground floor plan

Site plan

Cross section

by Architectural office Radko Kvet

Archeopark Pavlov

The Archeopark Pavlov combines contemporary audiovisual technology with traditional museum displays. The majority of the construction is situated underground, with just the white concrete towers projecting above ground. The main exhibition area – as well as the administrative, technical and social areas – is hidden in the hillside. The skylight tower projects to the exterior, as does the conical entrance and the lookouts to Děvičky and the lake below. The intention is for the building to be reminiscent of the shape of a cave. Regarding the materials, up-to-date means are used to express monolithic reliefs with concrete, oak wood and glass. The entrance area is multifunctional: It is also used for open-air activities, which accommodate the spatial and functional use of the area while subtly contributing to the scenery under the Děvín hill.

Location: Pavlov, Czech Republic
Architect: Architectural office Radko Kvet
Year of Completion: 2016
Type of Concrete: in-situ concrete

The Archeopark Pavlov with the Děvín hill in the background

Exhibition area detail

Wood and concrete complement each other

Exhibition area

Děvín hill and the Archeopark Pavlov

by Morger Partner Architekten

Residential / Commercial Building Bâleo

In the north of Basel, the new residential quarter Erlenmatt has been developed with attractive green spaces, schools and kindergardens, as well as shopping and dining options. The Bâleo building surrounds two spacious courtyards and offers 317 apartments next to retail and commercial areas such as an underground mall. The various apartment types adapt to the different conditions in the building.

Location: Erlenmatt, Basel, Switzerland
Architect: Morger Partner Architekten
Year of Completion: 2019
Type of Concrete: prefabricated concrete

Those lining the main street are ventilated via a green patio opposite the road, which also keeps the noise outside. The atelier apartments on the ground floor combine work and private life in a symbiotic room structure and contribute to the social interaction in the quarter. The concave form of the façade with its prefabricated concrete elements adds rhythm to the large volume. The color scheme is inspired by the red sandstone typical for Basel.

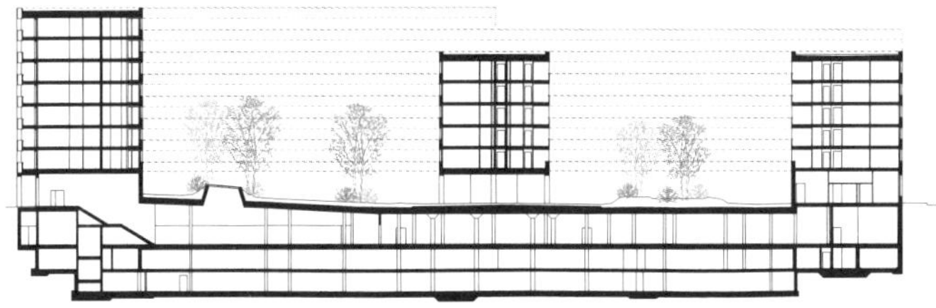

Cross section

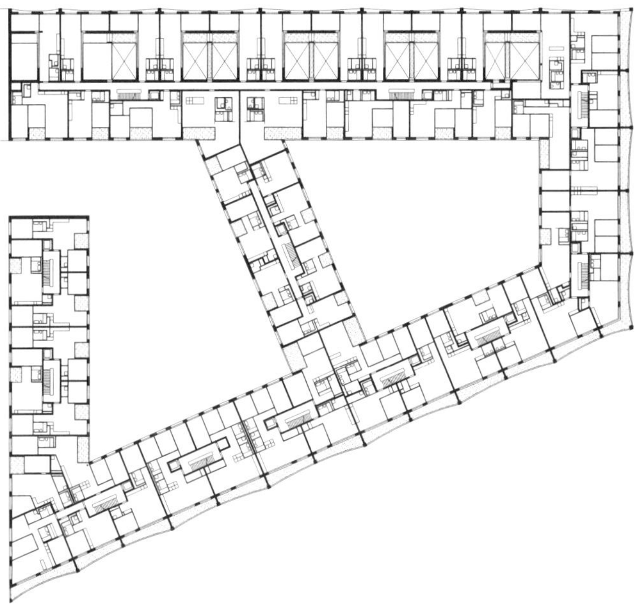

Second floor plan

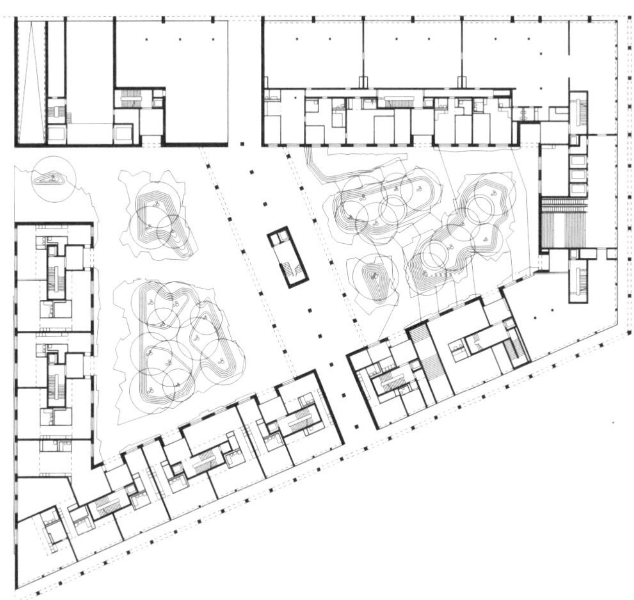

Ground floor plan

Atrium apartment with green patio

Façade detail

Atelier apartment ground floor

Southeast façade

Green courtyard

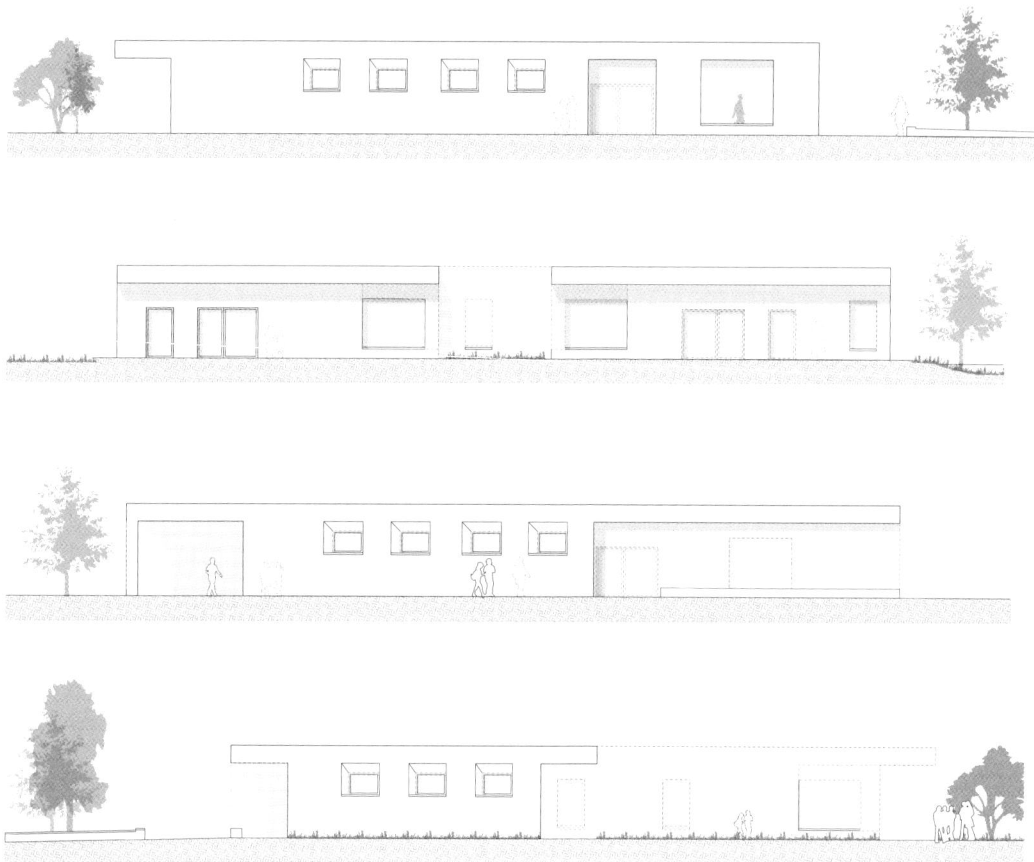

Elevations

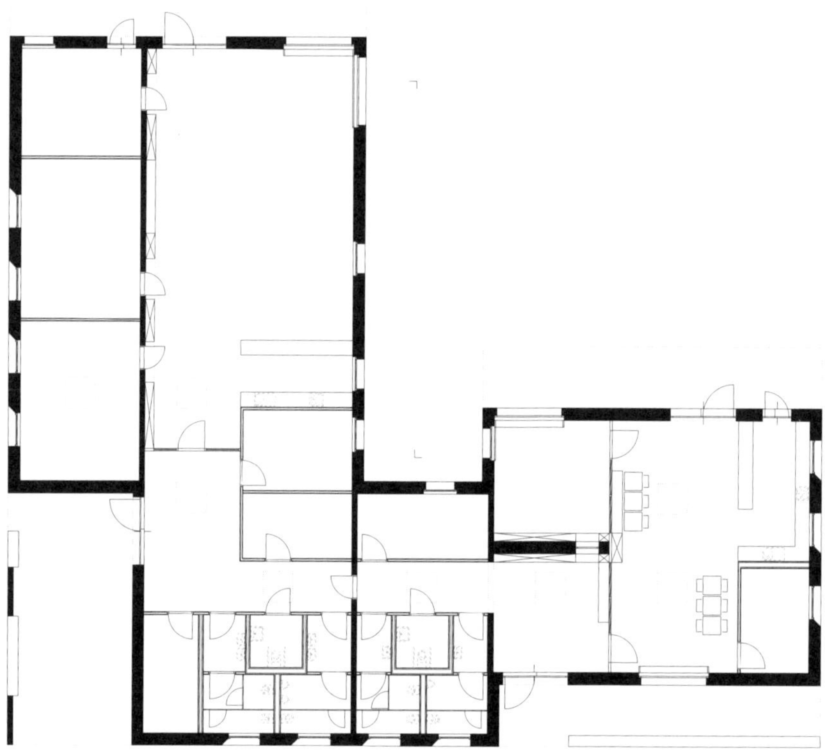

Ground floor plan

by GRUBER + POPP ARCHITEKTEN

Betonoase

The name of the new building located in Berlin-Lichtenberg reflects its program, the "Betonoase", which means concrete oasis, is the first public building with warm walls formed by infra-lightweight concrete. The house used for youth clubs and a family center consists of a monolithic wall, separating and simultaneously connecting the inner part of the building with the surrounding landscape. To realize the main idea behind the building, namely gaining an atmosphere of privacy in a living environment characterized by high-rise buildings, a stepwise translation between public and private spaces was needed. This concept was implemented by a public forecourt, a semi-public entrance area and the private rooms in the building.

Location: Berlin, Germany
Architect: GRUBER + POPP ARCHITEKTEN
Year of Completion: 2018
Type of Concrete: infra-lightweight concrete

Façade with forecourt

Façade detail

Window details

Art in the building

Interior

by hauschild + siegel architecture

Ohboy Hotel

The Ohboy hotel's design was inspired by the city surrounding it. A city that has become more biker-friendly and ecological, hence the goal was to create a project for a sustainable and urban lifestyle. The hotel houses 51 apartments and 33 hotel rooms.

Location: Malmö, Sweden
Architect: hauschild + siegel architecture
Year of Completion: 2017
Type of Concrete: exposed concrete

The essential influence for the design of the hotel are bicycles. In general, the design was meant to be spacious, the interior has wide doors and extra parking areas and entrances, so a bike can be brought inside. The exposed concrete façade of the building relates to the skating park right in front of the hotel, and provides a quiet indoor environment despite the busy neighborhood. Concrete is also part of the interior design, as the walls are made of exposed concrete.

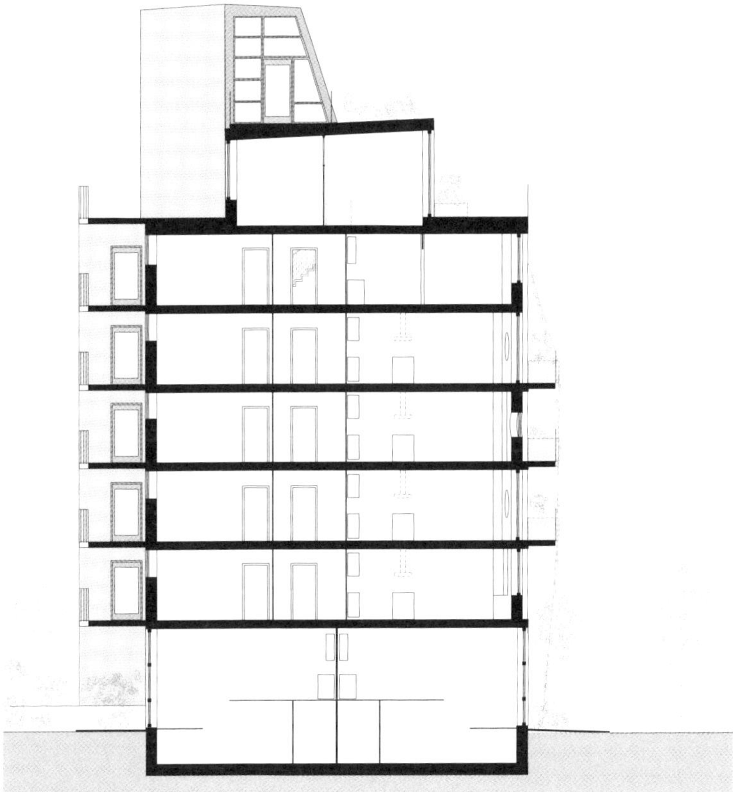

Cross section

Ground floor plan

Façade detail

Entrance area

Entrance with the overlying balconies

Entrance of a ground floor apartment

Living area

Working space

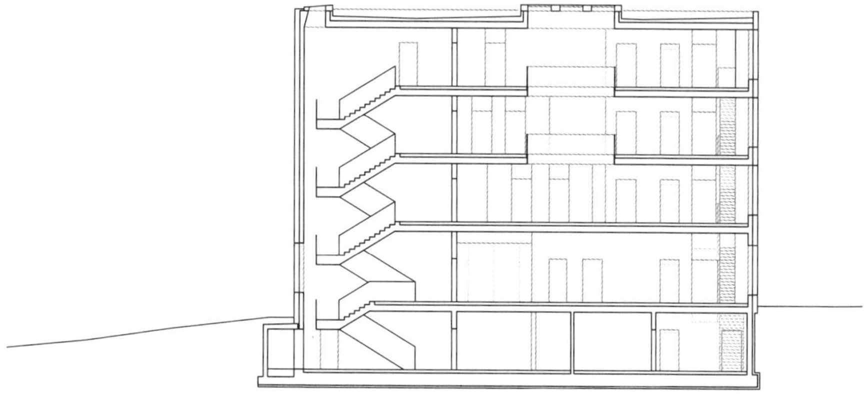

Cross section

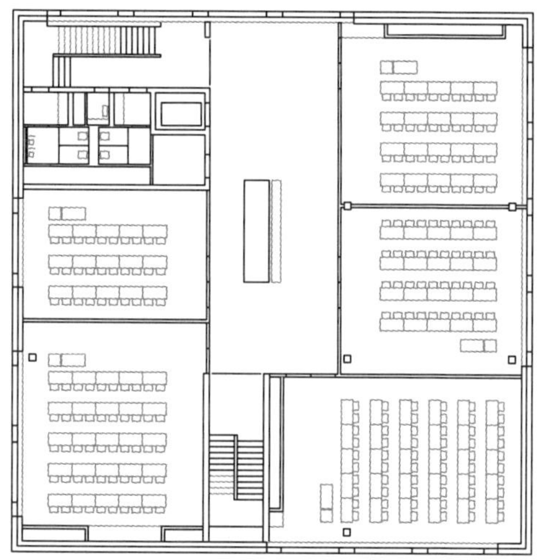

First floor plan

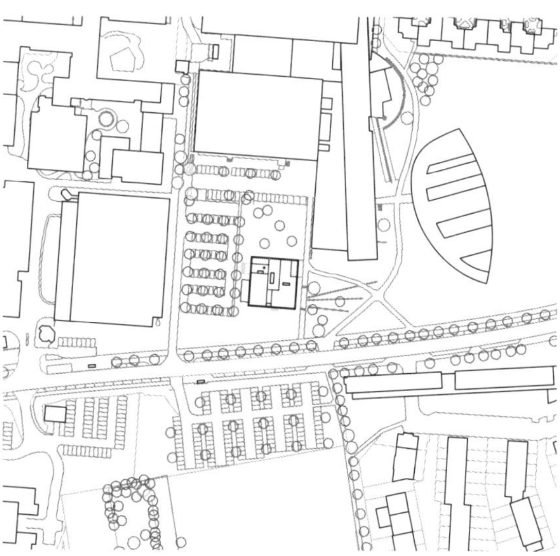

Site plan

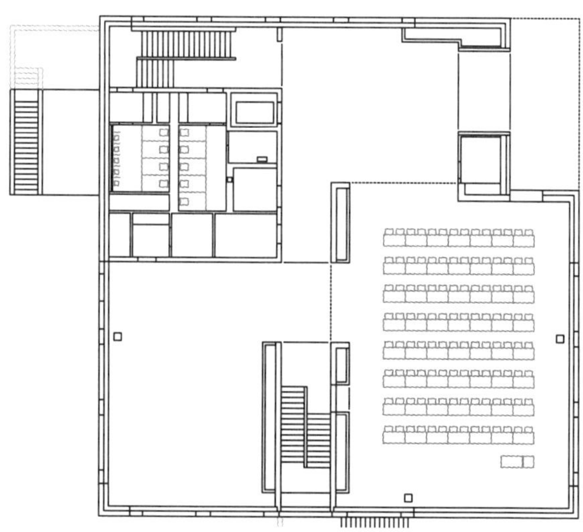

Ground floor plan

by Simon Freie Architekten

HdM, Seminar Building

The solitary cube with its four floors offers another 1,850 square meters to the quickly growing university of media (Hochschule der Medien, HdM). Next to seminar and project rooms the new building provides a lecture hall, a photo studio and the multi-functional creativity lab. The western open-air area, which is also used as a green classroom connects the inside with the surrounding nature. Apart from the exceptional cube shape, the building defines itself through simple, timeless elegance. The load-bearing façade is created with ready-mix concrete sandwich elements. Big, prominent window openings create a special transparency which leads to a bright, friendly study atmosphere and allows a special view in the surrounding landscape. To gain an adaptable building, the walls of the seminar, project and office rooms are non-load-bearing and allow a flexible change of room structure and size.

Location: Stuttgart, Germany
Architect: Simon Freie Architekten
Year of Completion: 2016
Type of Concrete: ready-mix concrete

South façade

Major seminar room ground floor

Main entrance

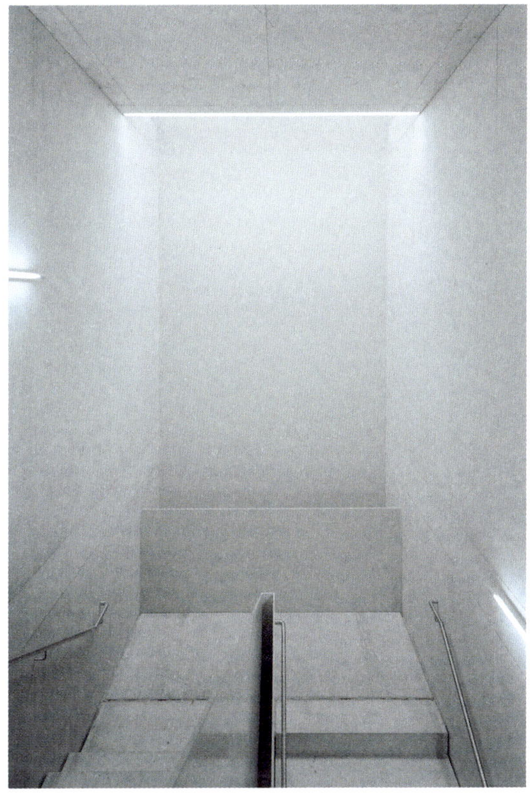

Staircase south

Seminar room first floor

by Klein Dytham architecture

SHONAN T-SITE

This is Klein Dytham architecture's second T-SITE bookstore project for Tsutaya, Japan's leading media and retail company. It is located two kilometers from the famous Shonan coast and the area's vibe influenced the project to become relaxed and approachable. Through a series of gateways and portals that were shifted along a central axis, it was possible to create small parks and natural entrances. The portals were shifted vertically and horizontally, to help modulate the architecture of the building and allowing light in the central areas. Tsutaya, the company's name is written in two kanji-alphabet characters – "tsuta" and "ya". "Tsuta" means ivy and "ya" means house, which lead to the ivy pattern on the façade. This was used to soften the exterior, and it also makes up for the lack of greenery.

Location: Fujisawa, Japan
Architect: Klein Dytham architecture
Year of Completion: 2014
Type of Concrete: precast concrete

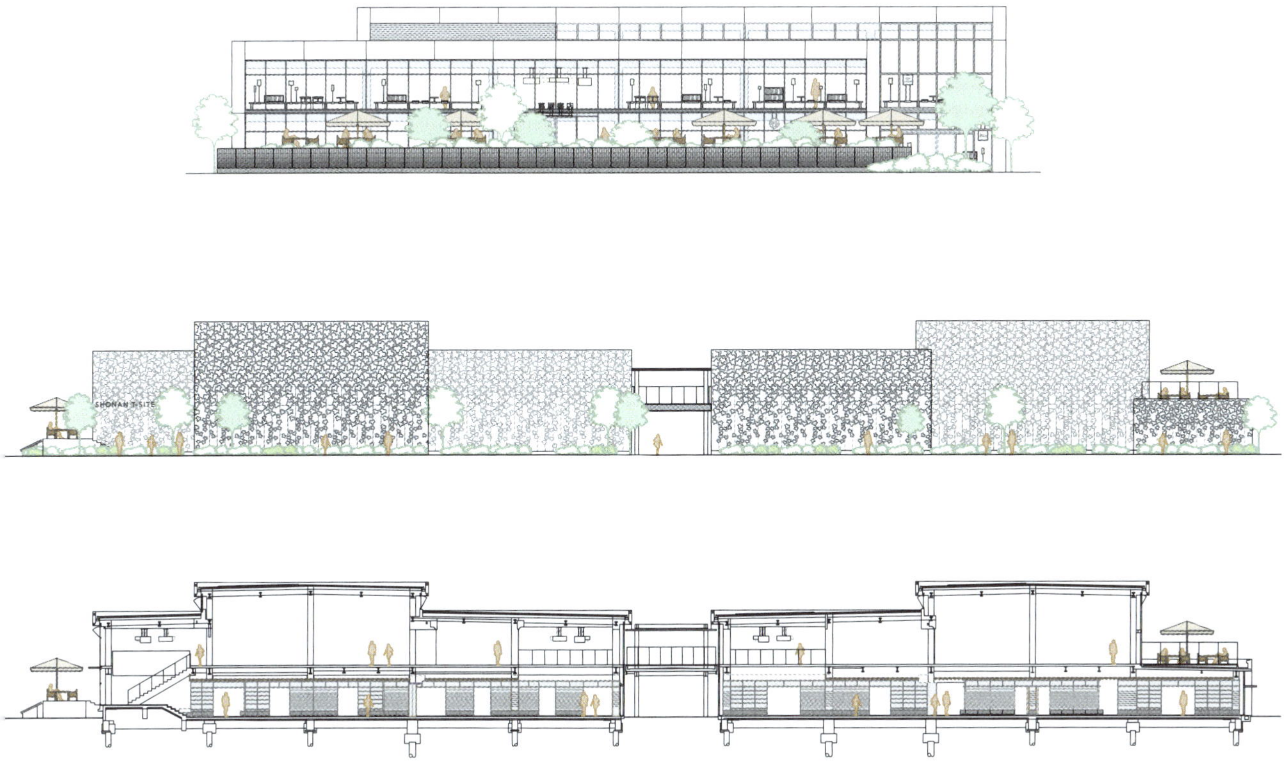

Sections and elevations

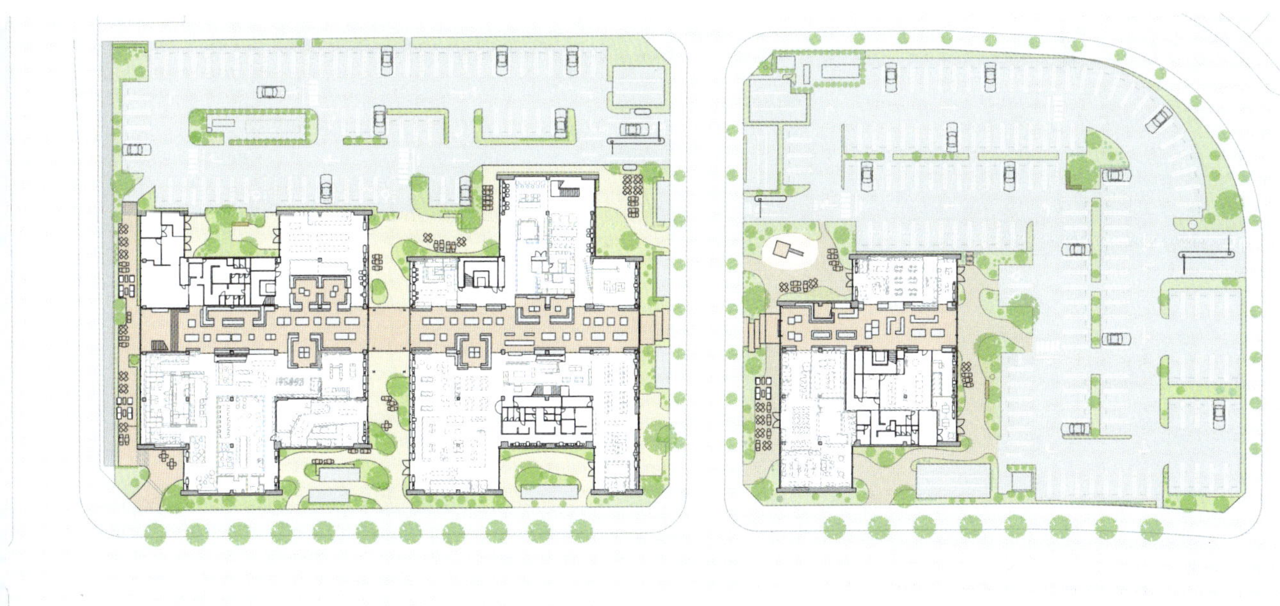

Ground floor plan

View from the parking lot

Magazine street

Façade detail

Shonan Lounge

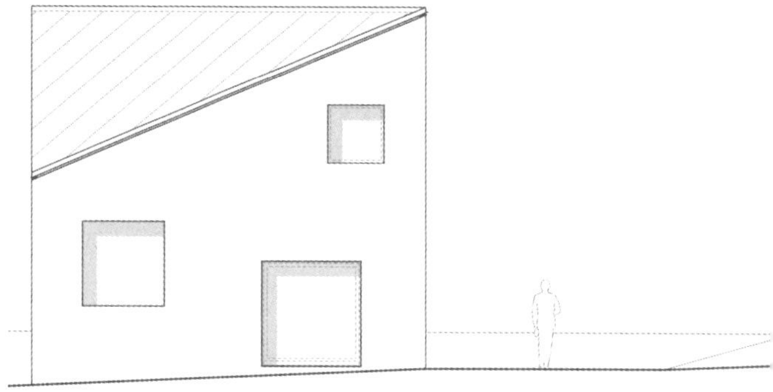

Elevation

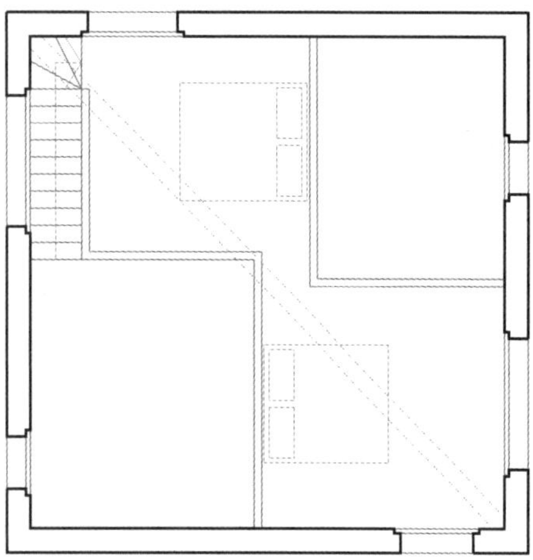

First floor plan

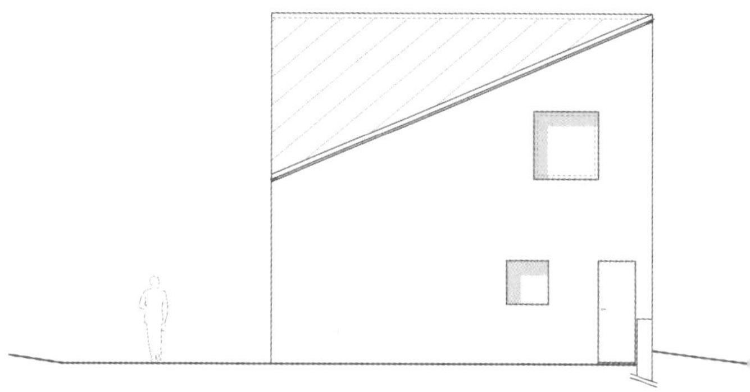

Elevation

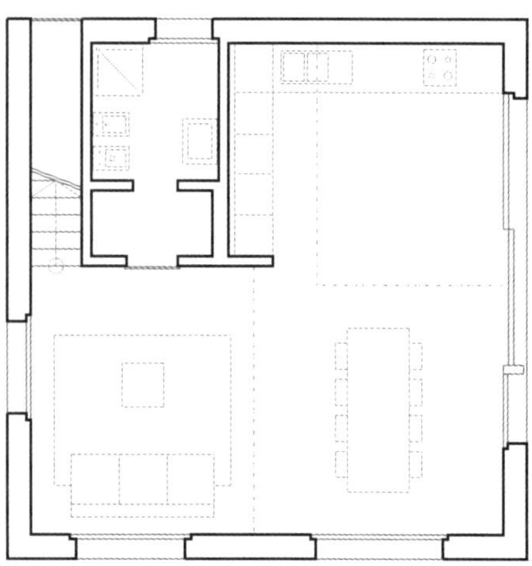

Ground floor plan

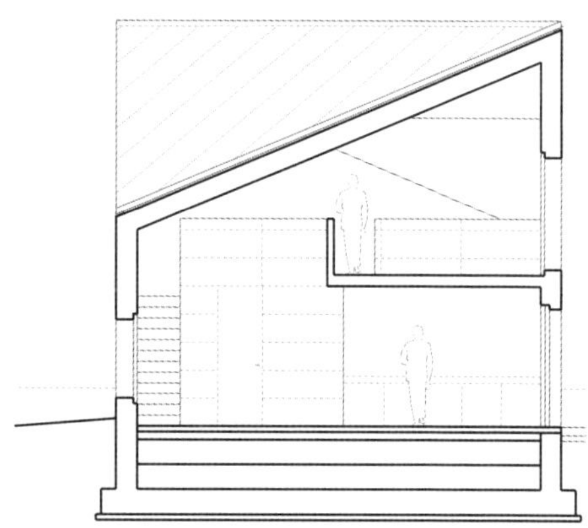

Cross section

by 35a studio

House R

This small holiday home is conceived as a single double-height volume: the open-space ground floor is divided into a large living area, a dining area and the kitchen; on the upper floor there are two bedrooms, overlooking the living area below. Characteristic of the house is the 45-degree rotation of the traditional roof cover, with the creation of four identical, trapezoidal sections. The large openings in each space ensure a continuous relationship with the surrounding landscape and immersing the entire house in light. The reinforced concrete, used to eliminate any structural element inside and reduce the construction costs, was placed using common yellow panels and leaving it internally exposed. Outwardly the façades are finished with a dark-gray, coarse-grained plaster, all the materials used follow the brutalist language of the entire work.

Location: Valverde, Italy
Architect: 35a studio
Year of Completion: 2017
Type of Concrete: reinforced concrete

East façade

View from the bedroom

Living room

Dining area and view of the double-height

Southwest façade

Garden view by night

by OIA OpenIdeas

Narmada Bio Chem HQ

Narmada Bio Chem Ltd produces fertilizers for the agricultural sector. With need to consolidate operations of three different locations into one, this project was seeded in creating an entity that would inspire trust in business partners and embody the company's growth. The design became an exercise in rational and optimum space planning on a tight, 570-square-meter plot. The architects revisited the modernist syntax, to articulate a clean built environment with good detailing. The core company business being related to agriculture, prompted the architects to think of a material manifestation that would be raw, close to the earth and rooted — culminating in concrete as the material of choice. Glass symbolizes lightness and transparency. Used as a counterbalance to the solidity of concrete and to make daylight a constant part of the internal spatial experience.

Location: Ahmedabad, India
Architect: OIA OpenIdeas
Year of Completion: 2019
Type of Concrete: in-situ concrete

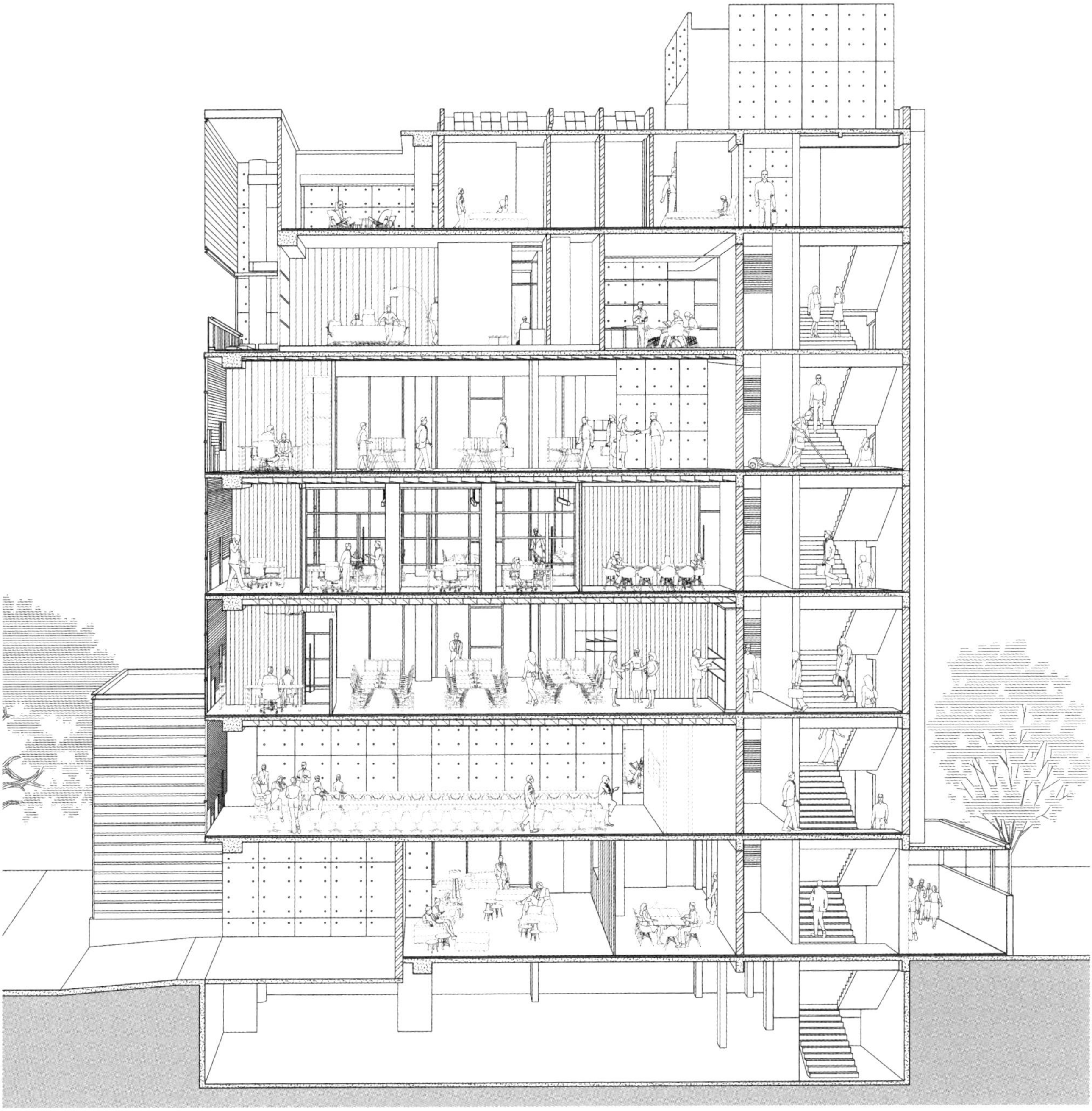

Section

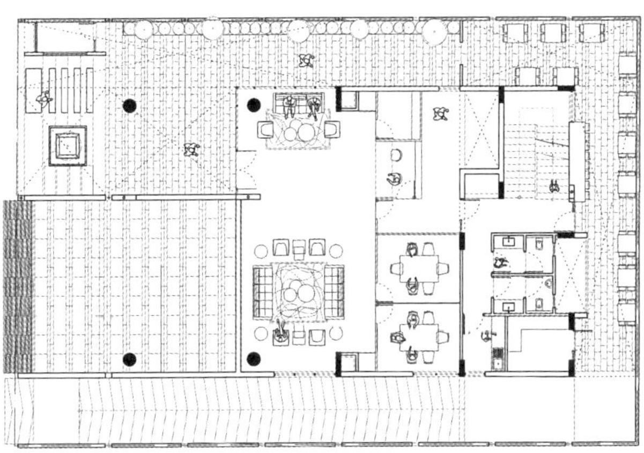

Ground floor plan

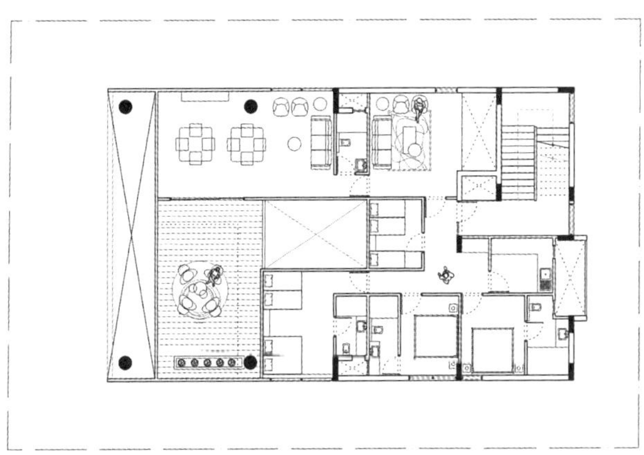

Sixth floor plan

Support on a glazed corner

Elegant volume with entrance

Seating area in front of exposed concrete

Open space on the sixth floor

Conference hall showing elegant simplicity

Lightweight and concrete go together

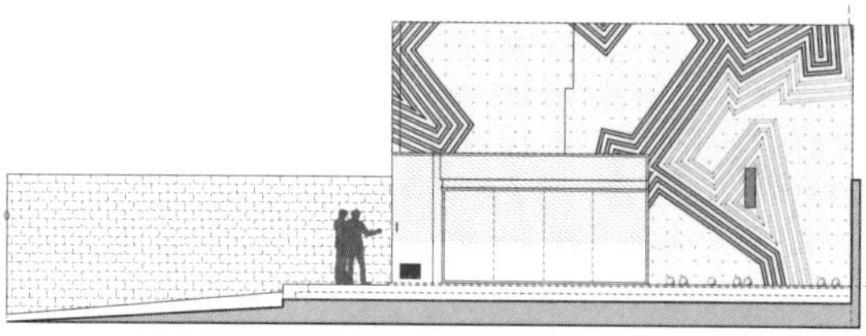

East elevation

South elevation

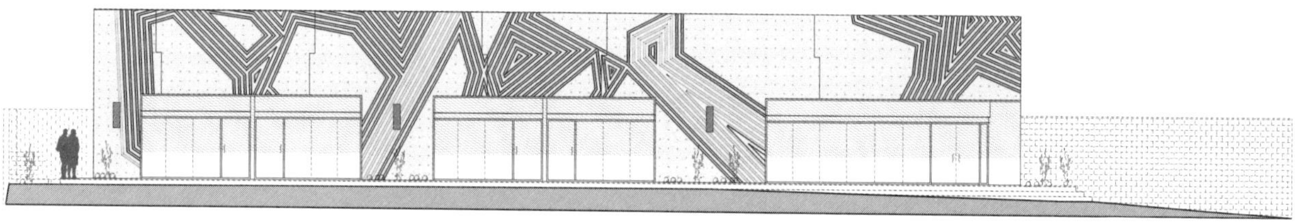

West elevation

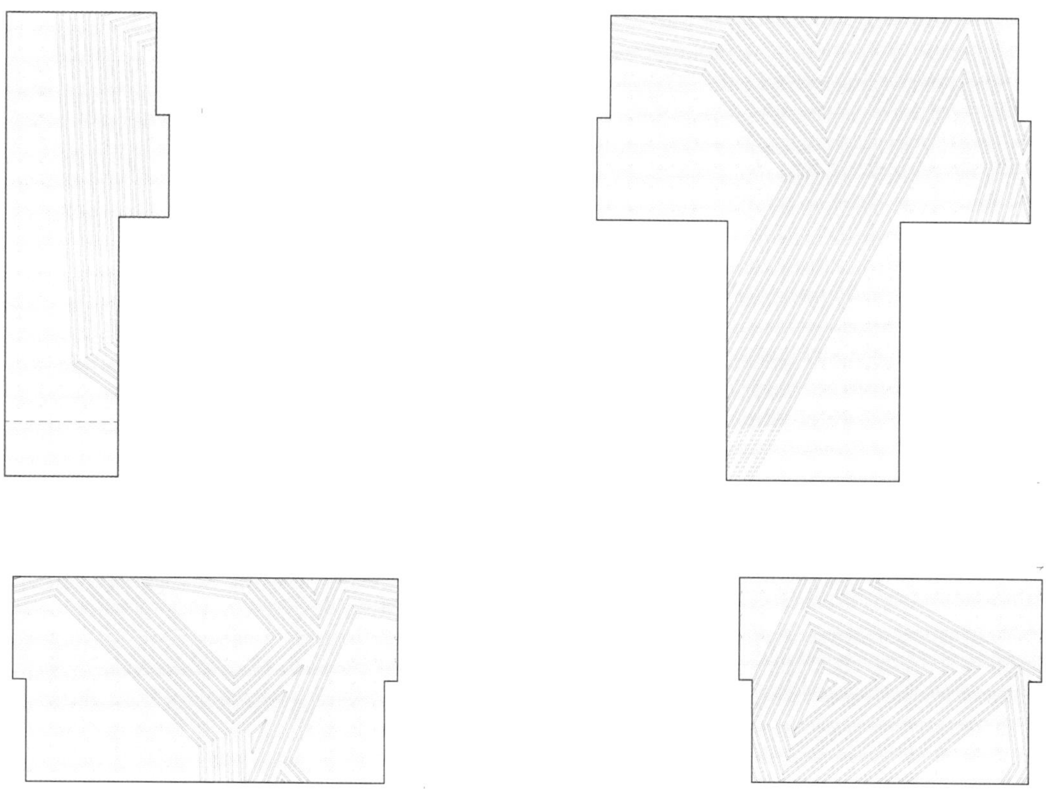

Prefabricated façade elements

by Jorge Urias Studio

Anapra

The Anapra neighborhood in Ciudad Juárez is a place with richness of textures and exposed materials, where the built environment can be seen as a reflection of its people's creativity portrayed in their unique construction systems. The goal was to create the design of a low-cost commercial structure with an open floor plan that could be redistributed as needed. A solid concrete mass emerges from the ground that is carved by a continuous pattern resembling the relationship among the residents and their environment. The raw materiality of the tilt-up concrete panels inherits the dynamic activities and informalities found in the neighborhood and creates an unprecedented structure which mirrors the qualities on site, becoming the building's skin.

Location: Ciudad Juárez, Chihuahua, Mexico
Architect: Jorge Urias Studio
Year of Completion: 2016
Type of Concrete: tilt-up concrete

West façade

Façade detail

Carved pattern

North façade

View from northwest

by Ruiz Pardo-Nebreda

Puma Energy El Salvador Headquarters

It is possible to access the plot through the interior street and the front gardens. The entrance hall is an area of spatial compression that acts by adjusting the scale to the user in such a way that the entrance to the building occurs through a more secluded area.

Location: Santa Tecla, El Salvador
Architect: Ruiz Pardo-Nebreda
Year of Completion: 2015
Type of Concrete: in-situ concrete

The lower block defines a space that establishes punctual relations with the exterior and it is shaped by walls with buttresses that support the roof slab. This configuration allows having continuous linear skylights parallel to the walls between the buttresses. At this level, the accesses and the program for external visits are resolved. A vertical void connects both blocks at their intersection and allows visual relations between different levels and programs. Structurally, the upper-level block is resolved by two parallel longitudinal gantries that make up two overhangs on opposite ends.

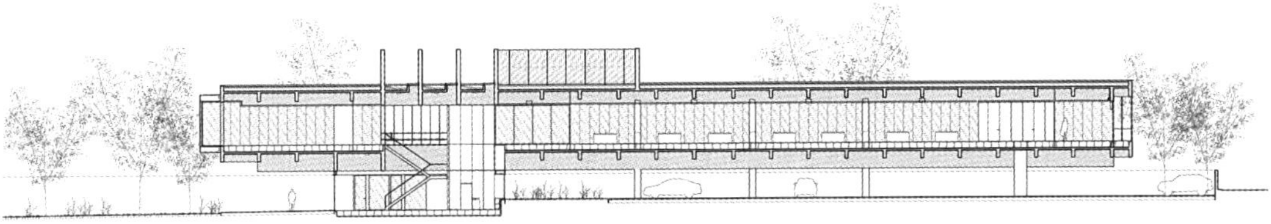

Longitudinal section

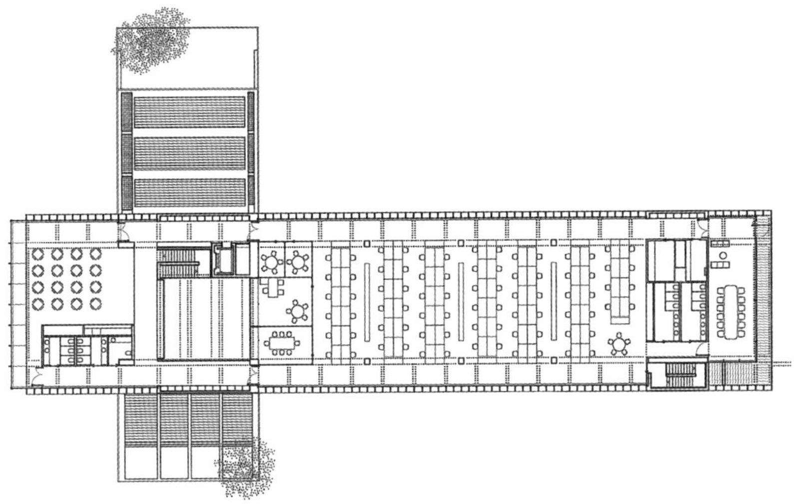

First floor plan

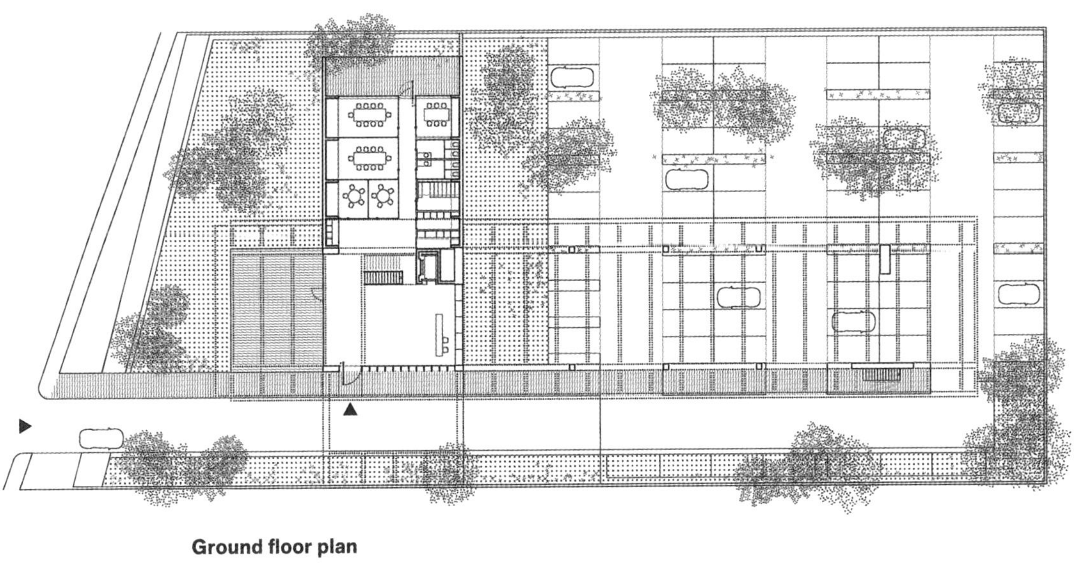

Ground floor plan

View from north

Concrete façade

Entrance hall

Entrance

The double-height is qualified by the zenithal light

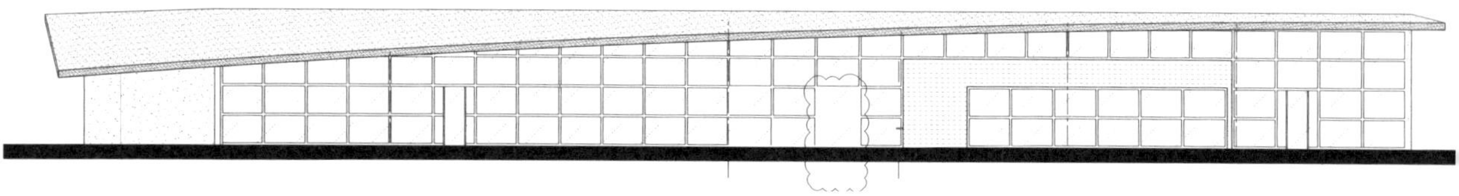

South elevation

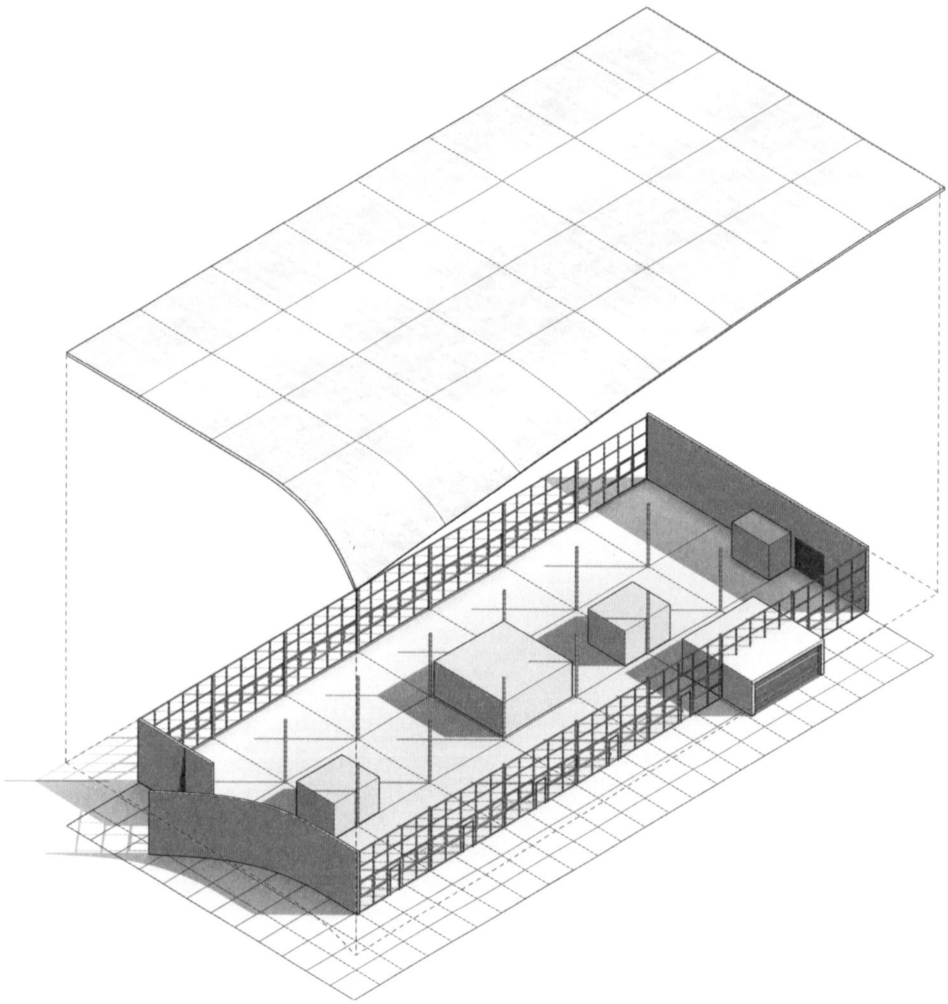

Axonometric plan

by Arquitectonica

Thomas P. Murphy Design Studio Building

The new studio building for the University of Miami School of Architecture provides a space conducive to learning and studying, but also serves as a teaching tool by illustrating some of the basic tenets of modern architecture. The warping corner of the roof folds over the southernmost tip of the building, shading the interior space from sunlight. The building has tall and flexible spaces, both indoors and outdoors. Narrow steel pipe columns support the ceilings to create a sense of openness and allow natural light to permeate throughout the building. The main entrance spills into an informal lobby and continues as a corridor that runs through the studios and out a garage door into the rear access road. Within the space, there are smaller volumes including the fabrication lab, which punctures the façade. The faculty offices are also moveable and can be redesigned by students each year.

Location: Coral Gables, USA
Architect: Arquitectonica
Year of Completion: 2019
Type of Concrete: reinforced concrete

Entrance area

South corner with the overhang canopy

Interior view

View from west

South façade

View from west with the building entrance

by Unterlandstättner Architekten

Monolithic Ensemble

Both houses, the main building and the guest house, were build with infra-lightweight concrete. The non-load-bearing inner walls with their opposing design raise a feeling for the architectural plan and constructional effort invested in the whole process of creating the houses. Smaller in size the guest house opens enough space to display the main building, offering a generous home to the inhabitants. Inspired by the local houses in the small town of Planegg near Munich, both buildings are protected from external insights but offer the residents a beautiful view of the garden area, which also offers plenty of natural daylight.

Location: Planegg, Germany
Architect: Unterlandstättner Architekten
Year of Completion: 2018
Type of Concrete: infra-lightweight concrete

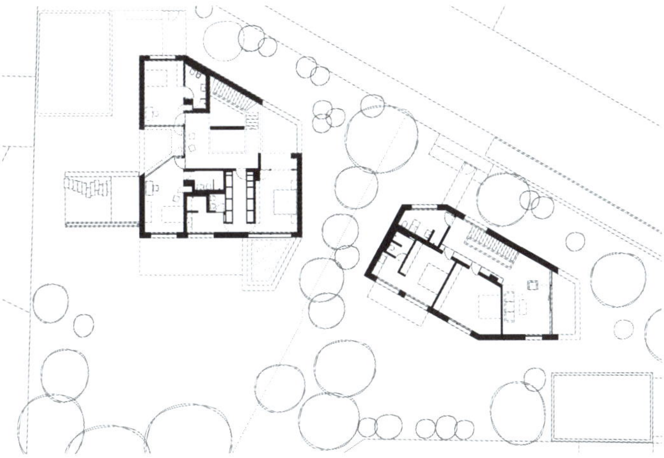

First floor plan

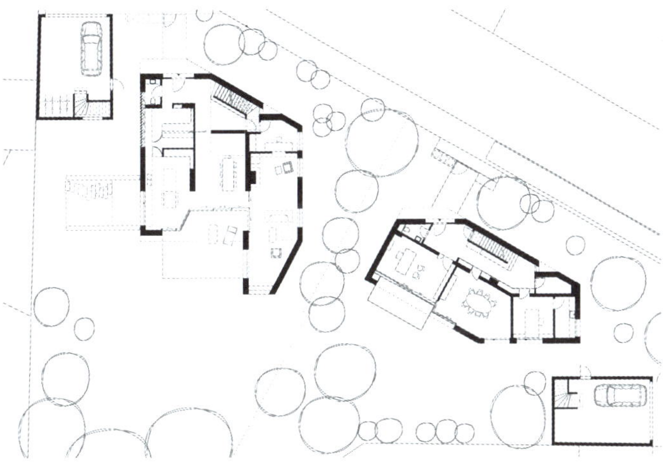

Ground floor plan

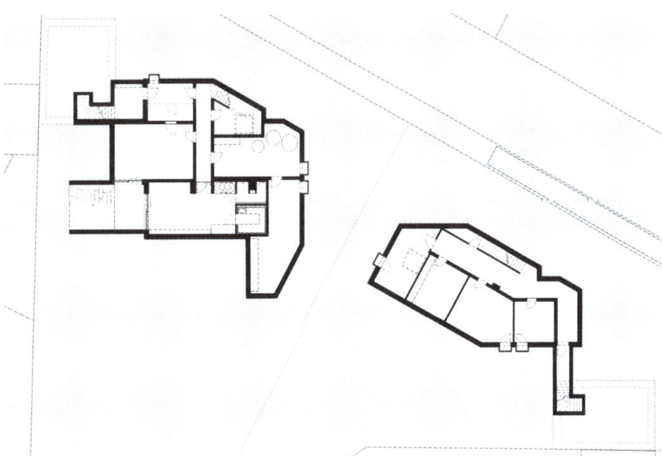

Basement floor plan

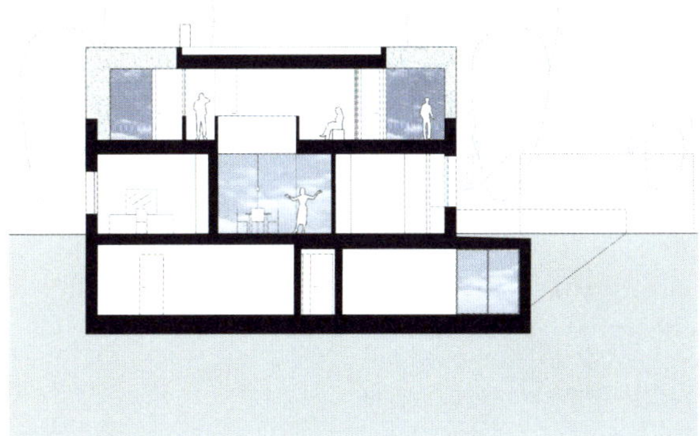

Cross section

First floor staircase house two

View from northeast house one

Dining room house one

Garden view house one

Street view house one and two

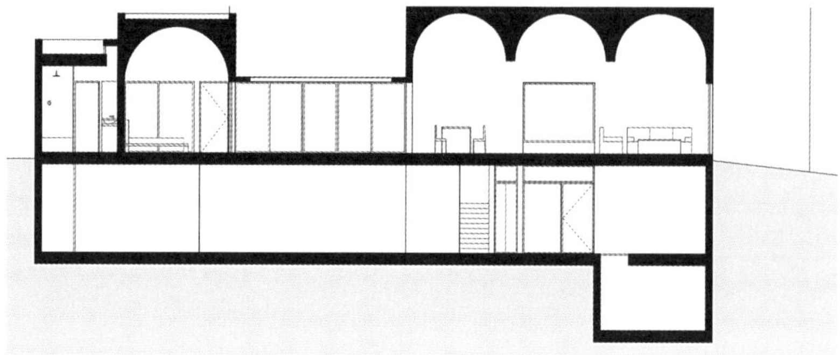

Longitudinal section

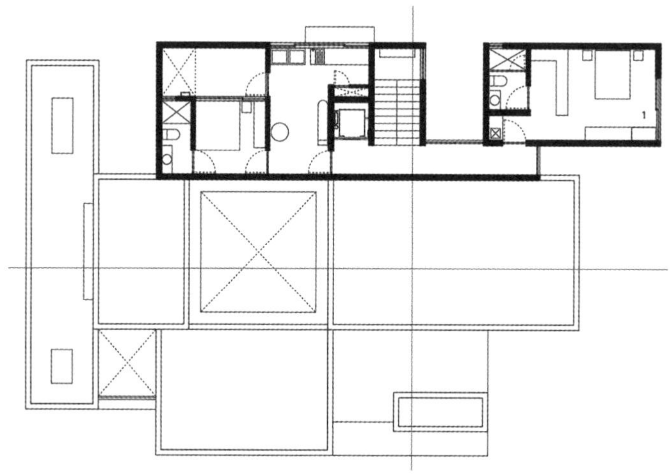

First floor plan

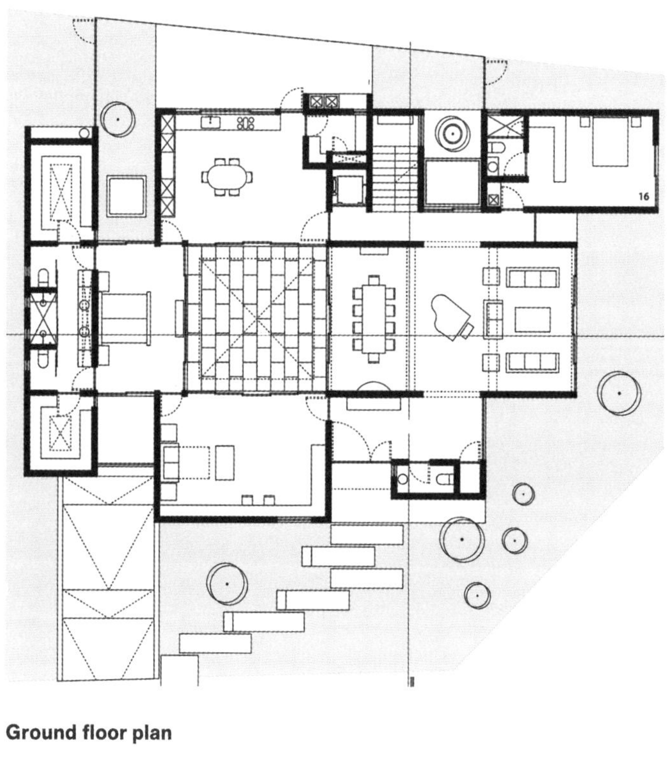

Ground floor plan

by SPRB arquitectos

Casa Acolhúas

As if it would the case of a precious musical instrument, the house is a robust wrapping that develops around the position of a majestic Bösendorfer piano. The main spaces are related to both, the central courtyard and the surrounding gardens, either for functional relationships or for comfort issues given the mild climate of Guadalajara. Introverted to its neighbors, it exploits its privileged position of contiguity to a public park. In contrast to the orthogonality of the floor plan, the section is contrasted with the different interior reliefs of the roofs in successive variations of scale, intimacy and spatial hierarchy. An honest materiality has been intended, both in its construction systems and in its finishes.

Location: Guadalajara, Mexico
Architect: SPRB arquitectos
Year of Completion: 2016
Type of Concrete: concrete with wooden formwork

Entrance view

Music room with a Bösendorfer piano

Patio

Hallway

Living room

Garden view

by studio mk27

Jungle House

The project is located in the rain forest, with a dense, mountainous vegetation. The introduction of this house to this landscape has the objective of optimizing the connection between architecture and nature, privileging the view looking out to the ocean and the incidence of sunlight in the internal spaces. The main volume of the house is elevated from the ground and seems built into the topography, therefore it projects itself out from the mountain. The contact elements between the slope and the construction were shaped to respect the existing land, thereby creating an organic interaction between nature and the architectural elements. The three floors of the Jungle House create a clear programmatic division for the project, this architecture allows the use of exposed concrete and wood, as much in the interior spaces as well as the exterior.

Location: Guarujá, Brazil
Architect: studio mk27
Year of Completion: 2015
Type of Concrete: exposed concrete

Cross section

Second floor plan

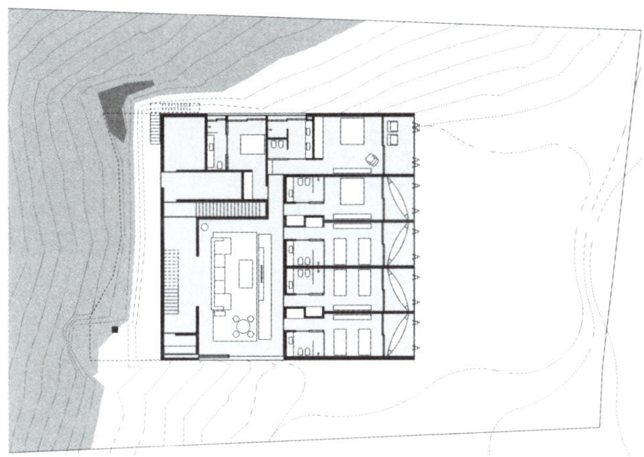

First floor plan

Ground floor plan

Terrace

Garden path

Internal circulation

Bird's-eye view

Living room

Outside space next to the living room

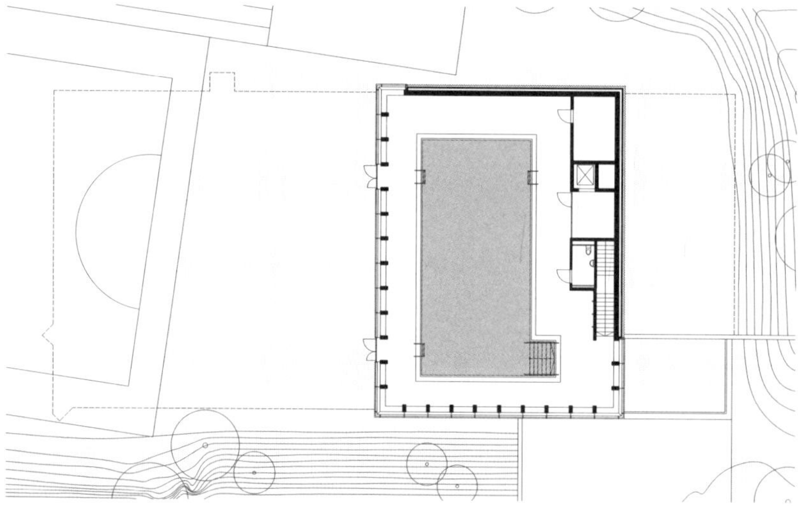

Ground floor plan

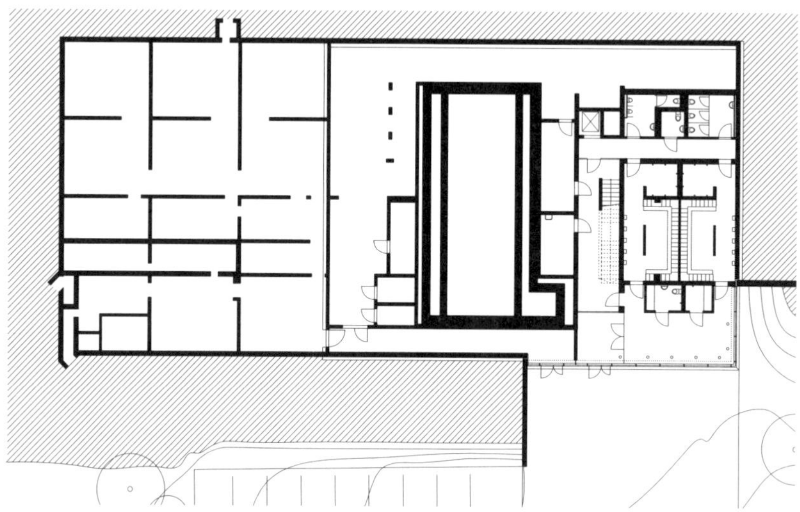

Basement floor plan

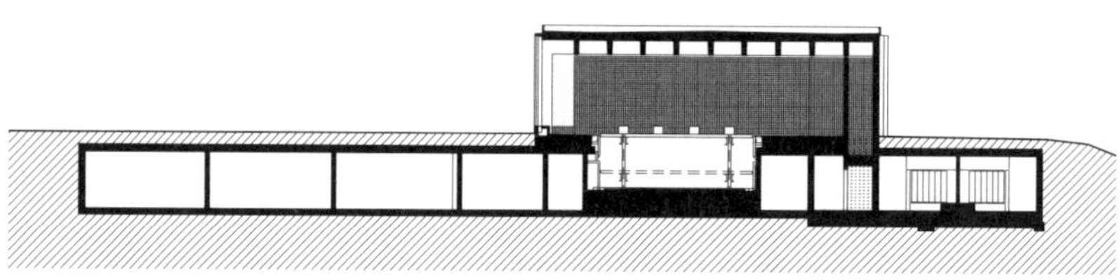

Cross section

by illiz architektur and AFRY Schweiz

Swimming Bath Allmendli

Two dark cuboids integrated into each other create the new building. A filigree, glazed façade covers the whole swimming bath being completed by steel and concrete columns in the interior. Between these pillars new seating possibilities are created, silver-gray benches form themselves matching the big concrete coffered ceiling. The swimming pool is at ground level allowing a great view at the Lake Zurich through the big glass front, opposite to this façade a wall with silvery-green and light pink wall panels creates a special atmosphere. In the lower part of the building these panels get darker, ending in a gloomy, deep green, associating the dive in a shady, clear lake. This lower part of the building also contains the entrance, technical facilities and locker rooms.

Location: Zurich, Switzerland
Architect: illiz architektur and AFRY Schweiz
Year of Completion: 2016
Type of Concrete: exposed concrete

Bathing area

Locker room

Staircase

North façade

South façade

by Zaha Hadid Architects

KnitCandela

KnitCandela is a thin, sinuous concrete shell built on ultra-lightweight knitted formwork, constructed at the MUAC museum in Mexico City. The textile shuttering of the formwork is comprised of four long strips ranging, each of the strips is a seamless, double-layered textile. The visible inside is an aesthetic surface that displays a colorful pattern and reveals traces of the supporting cable-net falsework system. The KnitCrete, introduced by the Block Research Group of ETH Zurich, is an innovative and cost-effective formwork system for the casting of double-curved geometries in concrete. The formworks use a custom, 3D-knitted, technical textile as a lightweight, stay-in-place shuttering, coated with a special cement paste to create a rigid mould, and supported by additional falsework elements such as a tensioned cable-net.

Location: Mexico City, Mexico
Architect: Zaha Hadid Architects
Year of Completion: 2019
Type of Concrete: hybrid lightweight concrete

Ground floor plan

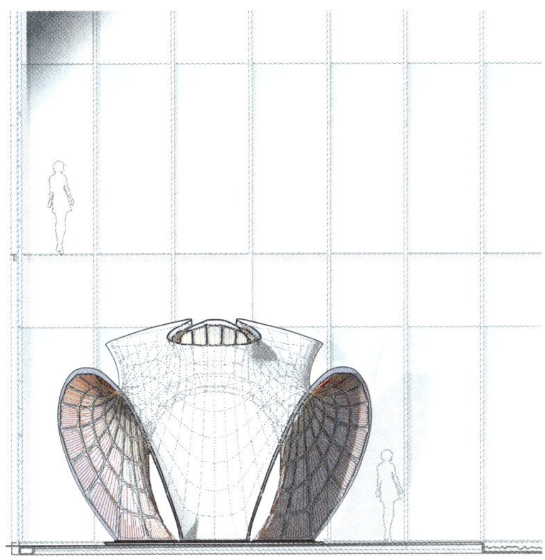

Elevation

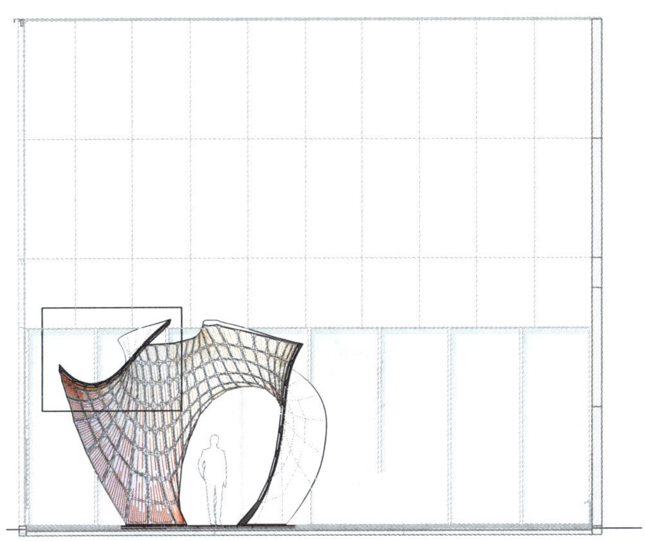

Cross section

Bird's-eye view

Inside detail

The soft textile interior of KnitCandela's shell and its concrete exterior is visible from all angles

The pattern enhances the visitor's spatial experience

Fabrication detail

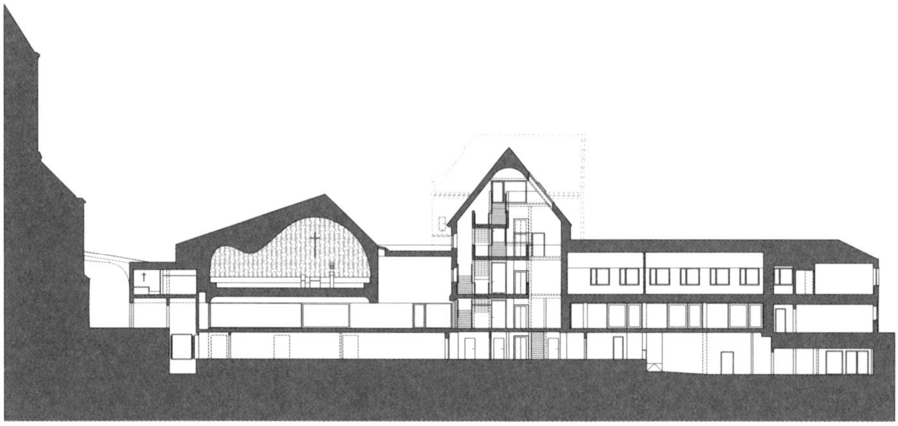

Cross section

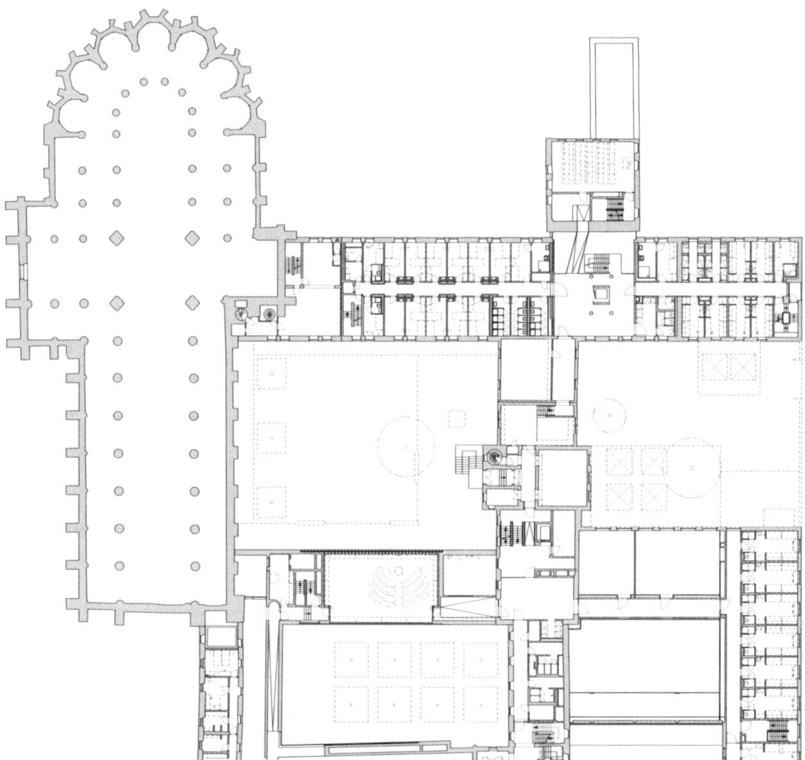

First floor plan

by gernot schulz : architektur

Christkönig Chapel Altenberg

The position of the new building presents the chapel with the challenge of an elongated spatial proportion in a north-south direction, contrary to the liturgical orientation to the east. The result is an asymmetrical room with two vaults, consisting of a firmly furnished main room and a deliberately empty side area. The liturgical area is centrally oriented towards an existing cross, important for the history of Haus Altenberg, which seems to float in the light of the openwork glass wall behind it. The modern tracery window follows building techniques handed down since the Middle Ages. However, the free arrangement of the tracery stones inside and their materialization from cast concrete elements are contemporary components of the façade.

Location: Odenthal, Germany
Architect: gernot schulz : architektur
Year of Completion: 2018
Type of Concrete: exposed concrete

Access to the chapel

Side aisle

Tabernacle

Rear façade view

Foyer Haus Altenberg

Main nave

by Jean-Pierre LOTT – architecte

Médiathèque de Vitrolles

The media library was built in concrete because of its plasticity, it gives shape and expresses abstraction. To create continuity the use of the same material allows freedom and integration of each part of the building. The building complex offers two faces: the ground floor located in alignment, entirely glazed, inviting to enter and a floor composed of a large sinuous veil of openwork white concrete, which expresses movement and lightness. The transparent base on the square gives the pedestrian the view of the entrance, the exhibition spaces, the cafe, the auditorium, bringing the building out of its frame. The cantilevered floor protects the consultation spaces on the upper floor from direct sunlight. Here, fluidity and light were the main themes.

Location: Vitrolles, France
Architect: Jean-Pierre LOTT – architecte
Year of Completion: 2017
Type of Concrete: in-situ concrete

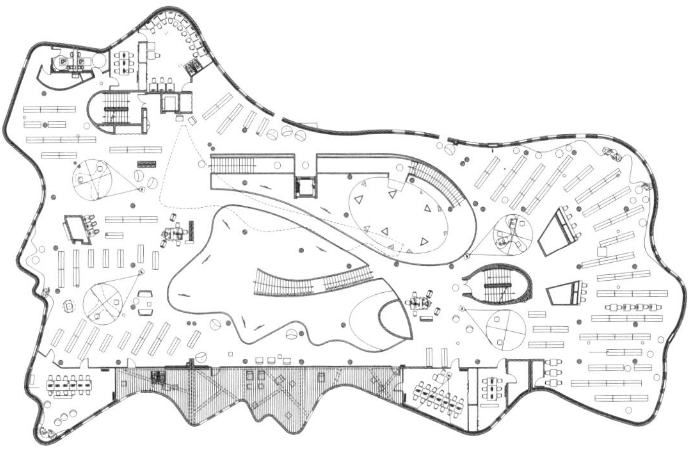

First floor plan

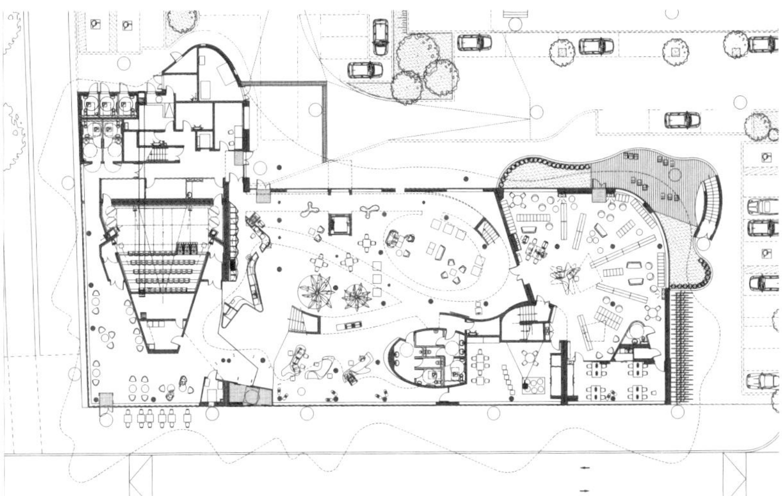

Ground floor plan

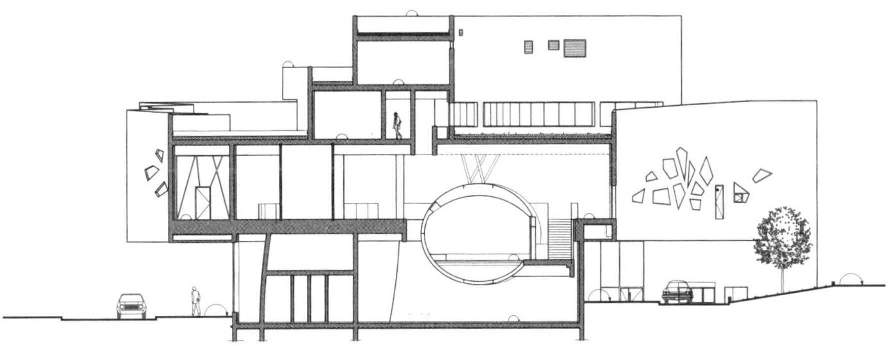

Cross section

Square view

Interior view from the entrance

Façade detail

Terrace first floor

Interior view of the story room

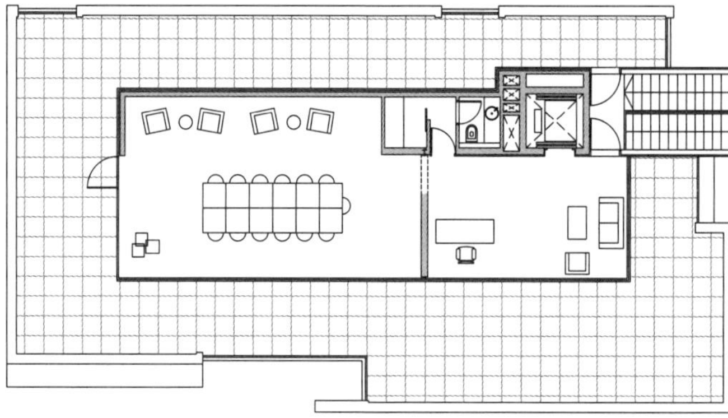

Second floor plan

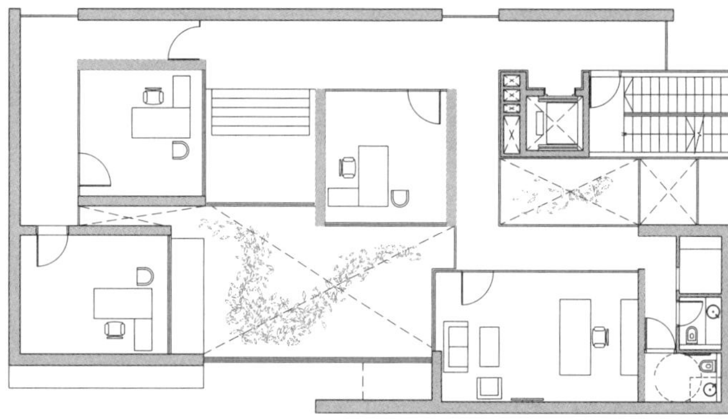

First floor plan

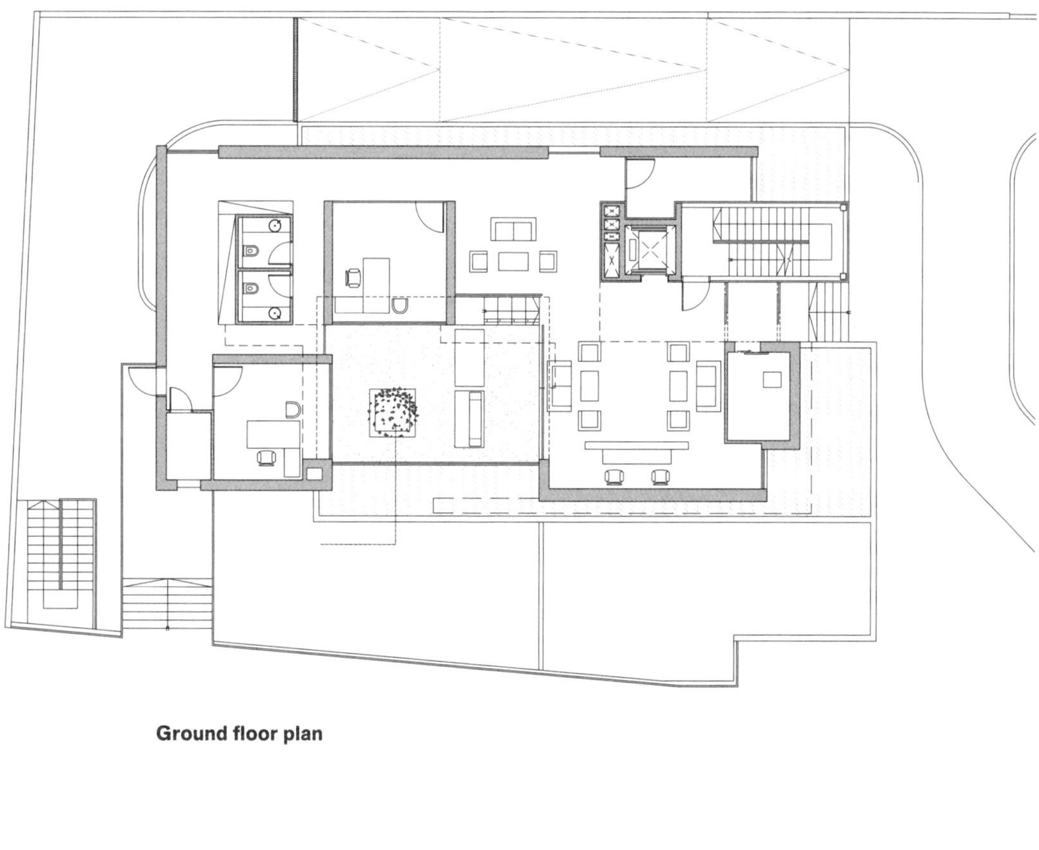

Ground floor plan

by Paradigm DH, Saja Nashashibi

Capital Bank Select Branch

The design concept "boutique bank" is a unique one that introduces a new approach to the bank experience. It is more private, luxurious, and tailored to the client's needs, combining the surrounding nature and the interior experience to make it more intimate and welcoming to the user. Translucent concrete was used for the first time worldwide as a self-supporting structure in the building's cladding. By using this material, the building sets a striking example of how external walls can solve the contradiction between massiveness and lightness through translucency. LED light panels were used on the handrail of the stairs, achieving a dynamic effect. Silhouettes of the people inside are projected onto the translucent concrete panels seen from the outside, enhancing the connection between the inside and the outside of the bank.

Location: Amman, Jordan
Architect: Paradigm DH, Saja Nashashibi
Year of Completion: 2018
Type of Concrete: translucent concrete

Exterior view during the day

Exterior plants shadows reflected on the translucent concrete of the staircase

View from north

Translucent and non-translucent concrete adjoining each other

Lobby with the inner court behind

Exterior view at night

by Killa Design

Office of the Future

The Office of the Future is the world's first fully functional and permanently occupied 3D-printed commercial building, completely manufactured using an additive concrete-printing technique, which took 17 days to print. This innovative construction technique cut labor costs by 50 percent and minimized site waste. The design used an 800 millimeters thick insulating cladding zone, fabricated using computer-controlled manufacturing techniques to improve energy efficiency in the UAE's hot climate. To maximize visibility and natural light, the interior spaces are shaded via projecting overhangs above the windows and optimized to completely protect the exterior glazing from direct sunlight. The complex radiates around a tree-shaded cafe courtyard. It comprises a partnership lounge and gallery for exhibitions, events and workshops.

Location: Dubai, United Arab Emirates
Architect: Killa Design
Year of Completion: 2016
Type of Concrete: additive concrete

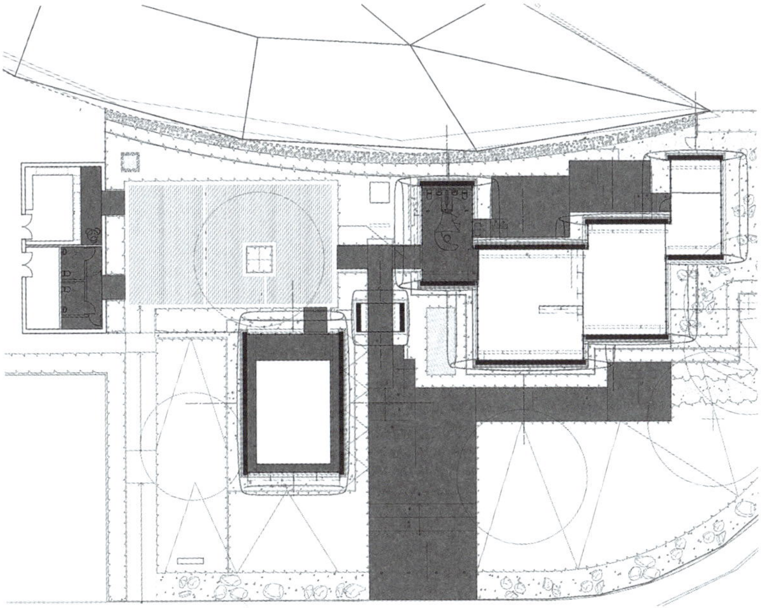

Ground floor plan with entrance at the bottom of the plan

The Office of the Future includes a gallery space, a multipurpose space and private meeting rooms

The Office of the Future: first 3D-printed commercial building worldwide

HH Sheikh Mohammed's 3-finger salute

A series of openings connect the interior spaces to the outside environment

The office complex radiates around a tree-shaded cafe courtyard

Reception area showcasing the additive concrete used in the structure's 3D-printing construction process

A knowledge hub for future generations of leaders

by + + Naso

Casa Martha

The family who lives at Casa Martha consists of the parents, who both suffer from physical constraint and their two grown-up sons. This situation led to the fundamental ideas of the house design, namely, to generate an accessible and clear circulation route, to promote the cohabitation of the inhabitants and to include variable spaces. The main volume with the common spaces, the kitchen, the dining room, the bathroom and two bedrooms, emerges from the rectangular plot. The nucleus of the house can be opened completely using sliding doors, allowing its inhabitants to immerse in the natural landscape surrounding them. The space on the second level can be accessed by an independent staircase, where the roof of the main house serves as a terrace.

Location: Malinalco, Mexico
Architect: + + Naso
Year of Completion: 2019
Type of Concrete: earth and concrete mix

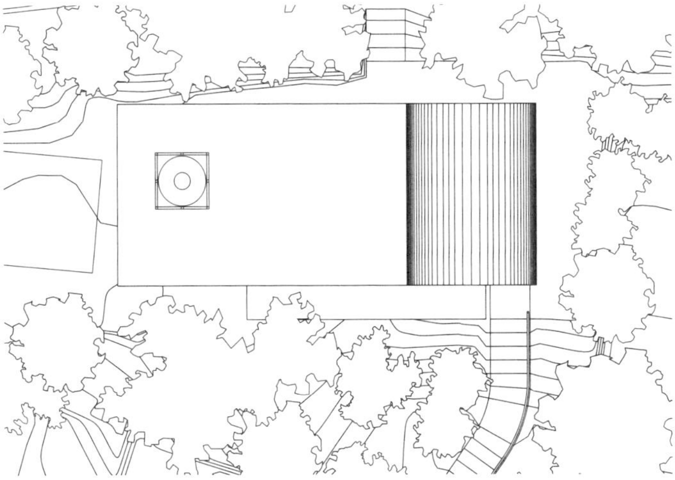

Second floor plan

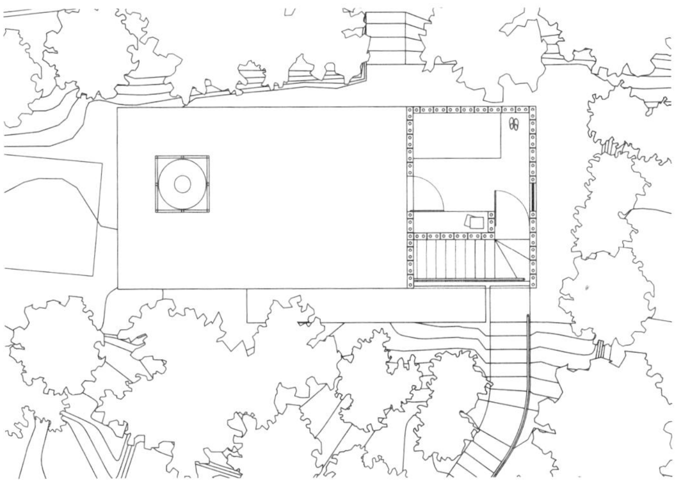

First floor plan

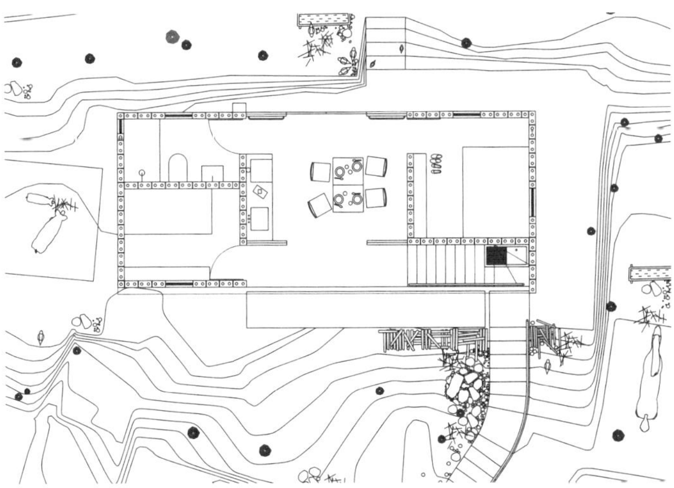

Ground floor plan

Roof acting as additional terrace

Kitchen area

Seating possibilities in the main room

Roof detail

Staircase leading to the roof

The sliding doors open the room towards the landscape

Garden view with the porch, the whole building was constructed by PienZa Sostenible

Architects Index

Picture Credits

Sireen Al-Khatib
(page 173 a. l., 173 b.)
Juan Pablo Allegre
(pages 156, 158 b.)
Ambiente Familiar
(pages 42 b. r., 43 a.)
Tonatiuh Ambrosetti
(pages 86, 88–89)
Aldo Amoretti
(pages 166, 168–169)
Matteo Aroldi
(pages 78, 80–81)
Stephan Baumann
(pages 75–77)
Philippe Block
(page 159 a.)
Alexander Blumhoff
(pages 99–101)
Zooey Braun
(pages 18, 20–23, 191)
Benjamin Cadena
(pages 41, 189)
Peter Carlsson
(pages 102, 104–105)
Andrea Carmignola Architetto
(pages 7, 115–117)
Lorena Darquea
(pages 143–147)
Gabriel Dvořák
(pages 91–93)
Assen Emilov
(pages 49–51)
Maureen M. Evans
(pages 182, 184–187)
Sandra Fauconnier / www.commons.wikimedia.org, CC-BY-4.0
(page 9)
Rafael Gamo
(pages 4, 125–127)
Rory Gardiner
(pages 10, 12–13)
Brigida Gonzalez
(pages 107–109)
Conné van d'Grachten
(pages 33–34, 35 a. r., a. l., 189)
Jesús Granada
(pages 128, 130–131)
Fernando Guerra FG+SG
(pages 6 a., 9, 44, 46–47, 148, 150–151)
hehnpohl architektur
(pages 52, 54–55)
Michael Heinrich
(pages 138, 140 a., 140 b. r., 141)
Ahed Hijjawi
(page 172)
Robin Hill
(pages 133, 134 a. r., 134 a. l., 135 a., 136–137)
hochstrasser.architekten
(page 35 b. r., 35 b. l.)
Florian Holzherr
(page 140 b. l.)
Hertha Hurnaus
(pages 152–155)
Ole Jais
(page 102)
Yoon JoonHwan
(pages 36, 38–39, 67–69)
Killa Design
(pages 183 b., 184 a. r., 184 b., 185 b.)
Philipp Kohler
(page 85 a.)
Wojciech Kryński
(pages 16–17)

Naho Kubota
(pages 42 a., 42 b. l., 43 b.)
Piotr Łatak
(page 15)
Frank Löschke
(pages 25–27)
Miami Focus
(pages 134 b., 135 b.)
Nacása & Partner Inc.
(pages 5, 110, 112–113)
Nabil Otteineh
(pages 171, 174–175)
Panchkon
(pages 118, 120 a.)
Paradigm DH
(page 173 a. r.)
Photographix India
(pages 120 b., 121)
Metipat Prommomate
(pages 28, 30–31)
Tim Van De Velde
(pages 6 b., 57–61)
Ruedi Walti
(pages 94, 96–97)
WAM
(pages 182, 184 a. l., 185 a.)
Simon Wegener
(pages 161–165)
Gustav Willeit
(pages 62, 64–65)
Yohan Zerdoun Photography
(pages 70, 72–73, 83–84, 85 b.)

Cover front: Yoon JoonHwan
Cover back (from left to right, from above to below):
Zooey Braun, Aldo Amoretti, Robin Hill, Gabriel Dvořák

Imprint

The Deutsche Nationalbibliothek lists this publication in the Deutsche Nationalbibliografie; detailed bibliographic data are available on the Internet at http://dnb.dnb.de

ISBN 978-3-03768-264-7

www.braun-publishing.ch

1st edition 2021

Editor: Editorial office van Uffelen
Editorial staff and layout: Leon Aickelin, Linda Gross, Alessya-May Lallo
Graphic concept: Ultrapaper – creative Studio
Reproduction: Bild1Druck GmbH, Berlin